Stephen King:
Uncollected, Unpublished
– 2014 Update

By
Rocky Wood

Overlook Connection Press
- 2014 -

Overlook Connection Press
PO Box 1934
Hiram, Georgia 30141

OverlookConnection.com
StephenKingCatalog.com
overlookcn@aol.com

First Trade Paperback edition
ISBN: 978-1-62330-052-4

E-book:
ISBN: 978-1-62330-053-1

Discover more about author Rocky Wood and his other publications on
Stephen King, graphic novels, et el at his official web presence here:
www.rockywoodauthor.com

Table of Contents

Introduction

In 2006 Cemetery Dance published the First Edition of my ground-breaking work, *Stephen King: Unpublished, Uncollected.* Four years of research had resulted in a book that identified some 51 works by Stephen King that had not been published and a further 46 that had been published but not gathered in one of his fiction collections. That book and each subsequent edition exclusively published a complete chapter from King's unpublished novel, *Sword in the Darkness* and reprinted an obscure poem, *Dino.*

By the time the Fourth Edition was published by the Overlook Connection Press in 2012 research had uncovered many more unpublished works. King had also published the collections *Just After Sunset* and *Full Dark, No Stars.* At that time there were 54 unpublished and 54 uncollected works. Each is described fully in that Fourth Edition, including advice to readers as to how (and if) they might obtain a copy.

This *2014 Update* reveals my latest research, often with the gracious input of Stephen King. Many mysteries have been cleared up and more unpublished works identified. In many cases Steve kindly provided commentary and information, which is published here for the first time. Of course, as we investigate the past, King writes in the present and has published a number of short stories that have yet to be collected. Including material in this *2014 Update* the count is now at 58 *unpublished* and 61 *uncollected* works of fiction by Stephen King!

As you read through the latest research gathered here you will find full detail about:
- A poem lost since King's college days
- Two unpublished short stories from the 1970s
- A story that won King a prize (and a lecture) when he was in High School
- Two lost stories from King's fan fiction days
- A play he wrote when he was 12 for his boy scout troop

Important updates are provided to information about these previously known works – *After the Play*; King's senior Class Day play (including its title, content, and comments from King); and the story

King wrote in fifth grade about his classmates being taken hostage.

A number of stories King is rumored to have written are dealt with.

Some obscure stories have been republished in easy to access form and that information is provided for readers.

A centerpiece of this Update is the full description of a lengthy busted novel – *Phil* and *Sundance*. In addition a new busted story that appeared to have great promise is described.

The latest published but uncollected works are analyzed, including:

- *A Face in the Crowd*
- *Afterlife*
- *Bad Little Kid*
- *Batman and Robin Have an Altercation*
- *11/22/63 – Final Despatch*
- *In the Tall Grass*
- *The Rock and Roll Dead Zone*; and
- *Summer Thunder*

All this new information has been discovered in just two years, proving again how prolific King is – in the present, as well as the past!

Update to the *Introduction*

This section updates material in the Introduction to the Fourth Edition of *Stephen King: Uncollected, Unpublished.*

The Bram Stoker Awards® for Superior Achievement have been presented since 1987 by members of the Horror Writers Association. King has won the Novel Award for *Misery* (in a tie with Robert McCammon's epic, *Swan Song*), *The Green Mile, Bag of Bones, Lisey's Story* and *Duma Key*; Fiction Collection for *Four Past Midnight, Full Dark, No Stars* and *Just After Sunset*; Long Fiction for *Lunch at the Gotham Café*; Short Fiction for *Herman Wouk is Still Alive* and Non Fiction for *On Writing.* Through 2013 he has been nominated a further 19 times, the latest for *Doctor Sleep* (his son Joe Hill's *NOS4A2* was nominated in the same category - Superior Achievement in a Novel) In 2003 he received the HWA's Lifetime Achievement Award.

We now know of 58 *unpublished*[1] and 61 *uncollected* works of fiction by Stephen King.

The general King readership can easily access over 150 individual Works of Fiction, in some 46 published novels[2], with 109 shorter works compiled in his nine collections[3].

In total there are at least 289 separately identifiable King story-lines, including other fictional works such as poems and screenplays. When all the differing versions, variations and titles of these works are taken into account there are about 402 different variants!

King is famed (and sometimes brick-batted) for the sheer volume of words he produces. Many novels are in the high hundreds of pages, with three exceeding 900, epics in their own right. One mythology (*The Dark Tower*) is barely contained in eight novels, two novellas, a raft of related tales and a series of *Marvel* comic extensions.

---

[1] In making these calculations the seven stories from *People, Places and Things* are classified as 'unpublished', as they were produced in a self-published chapbook by King and Chris Chesley, rather than by an independent publisher

[2] Inclusive of *Revival* (2014)

[3] Inclusive of *Full Dark, No Stars*

Updates to: *Linking Stephen King's Realities*

This section updates material in the *Linking Stephen King's Realities* section of the Fourth Edition of *Stephen King: Uncollected, Unpublished.*

All true King fans note these many links between his works, often deliberately put there by King for the enjoyment of 'Constant Readers'. In a 2012 interview with *Entertainment Weekly* about *Doctor Sleep* King had this to say about the subject, 'My son calls those things Easter Eggs. There's a little *Salem's Lot* Easter egg in *Doctor Sleep*. I don't know if anyone will spot it or not but it's there. All of the books kind of relate to other ones. The only exception is *The Stand*, where the whole world gets destroyed. I guess it's sort of like Stephen King World, the malevolent version of Disney World, where everything fits together.'

The following stories have either been published or identified as newly discovered unpublished works since the Fourth Edition, and have been assigned to Realities as follows:

America Under Siege
Afterlife
Bad Little Kid
Batman and Robin Have an Altercation
Doctor Sleep
11/22/63 – Final Dispatch
A Face in the Crowd
In the Tall Grass
Joyland
Mr Mercedes
The Dark Tower
The Wind Through The Keyhole
Maine Street Horror
Batman
Phil and Sundance
The Rock And Roll Dead Zone
New Worlds
Summer Thunder

Update to *The Dark Tower* section

In 2012 King published an extension to the mythos, with a novella that falls mid-stream in the narrative (King described it as the Dark Tower 4.5), *The Wind Through Keyhole*.

In October 2005 King and Marvel Comics announced the Dark Tower mythos would be extended with the publication of an initial six comic arc (to be collected in a hardcover edition). A series of arcs were published from 2007 and can be also purchased in collected hardback editions. Readers should note the original comic 'arcs', while collected in the hardcover graphic novels, contain a lot of background material about the Dark Tower Universe that are *not* included in those collections. This background is described by King's former research assistant and writer of the comic series, Robin Furth. The comics and graphic novels may be purchased from specialist stores or on the internet without difficulty.

The series released to April 2013 when it went into hiatus (in reading order) are:

The Dark Tower: Gunslinger Born; The Dark Tower: The Long Road Home; The Dark Tower: Treachery; The Dark Tower: The Sorcerer (one-shot comic, not collected); *The Dark Tower: Fall of Gilead; The Dark Tower: The Battle of Jericho Hill; The Dark Tower: The Gunslinger – The Journey Begins; The Dark Tower: The Little Sisters of Eluria; The Dark Tower: The Battle of Tull; The Dark Tower: Way Station; The Dark Tower: Man in Black and The Dark Tower: Sheemie's Tale.*

Update to the Maine Street Horror section

Story: Primary Settings:
Batman — Lisbon High School
Phil and Sundance — Derry

New to: *The Lost and Hidden Works*

The following are new discoveries to be added to the *The Lost and Hidden Works* chapter. That chapter reviews the works of fiction that have never been seen by researchers and King experts, let alone fans. They have either been lost or King has held them so closely that they have not been read by anyone outside his inner circle. The search for 'lost' King work will continue unabated for decades. King himself still seeks the lost manuscript of *The Float*. The works covered here have either been completely lost; or it is known King holds them. Stories only 'rumored' to have been written or to exist are not surveyed.

The Arguments Against Insanity

King gave an interview to Powells.com in November 2006, in which he revealed a lost poem from his university days:[4]

Interviewer: 'The line of poetry that Scott writes in *Lisey's Story* is a beautiful line, and seems to sum up a theme you come back to frequently: that madness, insanity, is never very far away.' / King: 'It's actually a version of a poem I wrote in college. I looked and looked — you know how you do workshops, and they make offprints of material. I thought I had some offprints from that, and I didn't, and so I called the prof who taught the class, and I said, *Do you have any of those offprints?* He looked, and he couldn't find it, either. Really, all I remembered of the poem was the first line, "The arguments against insanity fall through with a soft shirring sound," and I really didn't have much of a clue beyond that. So I worked on it a little bit, and it actually worked better, because it was more specific to the book.'

When queried about this King responded: 'The title was "The Arguments Against Insanity." I remember a few lines that went something like,

"The moon,
a disembodied custard pie
floating in the sky."[5]

The fact that King wrote this poem while at the University of Maine dates it in the period 1966-1970.

The Insanity Game

Justin Brooks lists this as an early 1970s twelve page typescript manuscript in the second edition of his Bibliography.[6] When queried about this King responded: "If there was such a story, it would have been written in the 60s, and is probably not complete.

---

[4] http://www.powells.com/blog/interviews/the-once-and-future-stephen-king-by-jill/
[5] Personal correspondence with Rocky Wood, 6 January 2014
[6] *Stephen King: A Primary Bibliography of the World's Most Popular Author*, Revised Edition (Overlook Connection eBook, 2013)

I wrote a lot of stuff back then, Rocky, but a lot of it never got finished."[7]

The Null Set

Justin Brooks lists this as an early 1970s twelve page typescript manuscript in the second edition of his Bibliography.[8]

The Points Dig Deep

King Bibliographer Justin Brooks ran across an interview in *The Guardian* (a prominent UK newspaper), dated September 30, 1977. In it King is quoted as saying, "However, he did win a pen that didn't write, plus 10 dollars, for an essay in a competition in National Scholastic magazine..." When I asked King about this during a meeting in Atlanta[9] he told me the story was called *The Points Dig Deep.* He said he was about fifteen when he wrote it and it was not very good. It is set in the Old West just after the Civil War. The Sheriff of the town gets word by telegraph that the Confederacy has surrendered. So he decides he will need to lower the Confederate flag flying over the town and raise the United States flag, in recognition that the War is over. But a mob forms in opposition and a man shoots him in the chest, which King described as a downer ending. He was attending Lisbon High School when he entered the competition and they were notified he had won the prize. He was called to the Principal's office, where he expected to be congratulated. The Guidance Counselor was also there and they asked him if he knew what plagiarism was. He said he did, copying someone else's work. They said if anything like that happened here we need to know - now is the time to tell us. Of course, King told them he had not plagiarized and they accepted that. He told me, "This is a problem with any writer with a young talent, people don't believe you can do it." When asked later if the story was published he said, "Alas, I only got an honorable mention for that story. And a pen that splurted ink all over my fingers. And a scary lecture about plagiarism. I have no copy..."[10]

[7] Personal correspondence with Rocky Wood, 10 April 2013
[8] *Stephen King: A Primary Bibliography of the World's Most Popular Author,* Revised Edition (Overlook Connection eBook, 2013)
[9] 4 April 2012
[10] Personal correspondence with Rocky Wood, 9 April 2012

Trigger Finger

A possibly unique piece of King Ephemera appeared on eBay in late 2012. The seller offered a one page flyer Stephen King had created to advertise stories from his cottage publishing venture, Triad Publishing Co. This was also the name King used to publish *People, Places and Things* (1960 and 1963) and *The Star Invaders* (June 1964). The flyer was posted to a fellow fan in New York and is postmarked 5pm, 6 September 1963 at the Pownal, Maine Post Office. It advertises three stories for sale – King's print adaptation of the American-International Film, *The Pit and the Pendulum* (King talks about creating and selling that tale in section 18 of the *C.V.* part of *On Writing* and there is a separate section about that tale in *Stephen King: Unpublished, Uncollected*[11]*); Trigger-Finger* and *The Undead.*

This is the full text of the flyer:

Dear Monster-Fan, / The crypt has just opened, and we here at Triad are letting out three of the most MONSTROUS tales to come your way in a blue moon. Here they are: / THE UNDEAD – a chilling excursion into the twilight world of Vampires, Terror, and... THE UNDEAD! Here's a sample: "Madly tumbling over each other, the kids piled back into the rod. One didn't make it. His head was split open like a ripe melon. The rod peeled out, spot-lighting one of the horrors in the glare of its headlights. It skidded..." 20 pages of TERROR! A Triad classic, only 35¢. / TRIGGER-FINGER – what happens when a trigger-happy intelligence agent invades Castro's Cuba in search of a beautiful U.S. space-scientist? PLENTY! Only 20¢. / THE PIT AND THE PENDULUM – this is NOT Poe's classic. It's adapted from the A-I shocker, starring Vincent Price. What's it about? Torture...premature burial...and the shambling horror that walked the darkened corridors of the storm-ravaged castle! Also, only 20¢. / These horrors are brought to you by TRIAD, INC. They are guaranteed to shock, or your money back! So get on the hearse, and read these terrors on the way to the crypt! / YES!! I wanto (*sic*) be scared outta ten year's growth! Send me the Triad Horrors I've checked. / THE UNDEAD 35¢ / THE PIT & THE PENDULUM 20¢ / TRIGGER-FINGER 20¢ / SEND TO: TRIAD PUBLISHING CO., C/O STEVE KING, R.F.D. #1, POWNAL, MAINE / (Enclose payment with money-order, please!)

---

[11] Fourth edition (Overlook Connection Press, 2012) - pages 60-61

When queried about *Trigger-Finger* and *The Undead* King said, 'I don't remember either one, which isn't surprising. Around the time I discovered *Famous Monsters, Spacemen, Creepy* and *Eerie*, those stories just poured out!'[12]

The Undead

A possibly unique piece of King Ephemera appeared on eBay in late 2012. The seller offered a one page flyer Stephen King had created to advertise stories from his cottage publishing venture, Triad Publishing Co. This was also the name King used to publish *People, Places and Things* (1960 and 1963) and *The Star Invaders* (June 1964). The flyer was posted to a fellow fan in New York and is postmarked 5pm, 6 September 1963 at the Pownal, Maine Post Office. It advertises three stories for sale – King's print adaptation of the American-International Film, *The Pit and the Pendulum* (King talks about creating and selling that tale in section 18 of the C.V. part of *On Writing* and there is a separate section about that tale in *Stephen King: Unpublished, Uncollected*[13]*); Trigger-Finger* and *The Undead*.

This is the full text of the flyer:

Dear Monster-Fan, / The crypt has just opened, and we here at Triad are letting out three of the most MONSTROUS tales to come your way in a blue moon. Here they are: / THE UNDEAD – a chilling excursion into the twilight world of Vampires, Terror, and...THE UNDEAD! Here's a sample: "Madly tumbling over each other, the kids piled back into the rod. One didn't make it. His head was split open like a ripe melon. The rod peeled out, spot-lighting one of the horrors in the glare of its headlights. It skidded..." 20 pages of TERROR! A Triad classic, only 35¢. / TRIGGER-FINGER – what happens when a trigger-happy intelligence agent invades Castro's Cuba in search of a beautiful U.S. space-scientist? PLENTY! Only 20¢. / THE PIT AND THE PENDULUM – this is NOT Poe's classic. It's adapted from the A-I shocker, starring Vincent Price. What's it about? Torture...premature burial...and the shambling horror that walked the darkened corridors of the storm-ravaged castle! Also, only 20¢. /

---

[12] Personal correspondence with Rocky Wood, 18 December 2012
[13] Fourth edition (Overlook Connection Press, 2012) - pages 60-61

These horrors are brought to you by TRIAD, INC. They are guaranteed to shock, or your money back! So get on the hearse, and read these terrors on the way to the crypt! / YES!! I wanto (sic) be scared outta ten year's growth! Send me the Triad Horrors I've checked. / THE UNDEAD 35¢ / THE PIT & THE PENDULUM 20¢ / TRIGGER-FINGER 20¢ / SEND TO: TRIAD PUBLISHING CO., C/O STEVE KING, R.F.D. #1, POWNAL, MAINE / (Enclose payment with money-order, please!)

When queried about *Trigger-Finger* and *The Undead* King said, 'I don't remember either one, which isn't surprising. Around the time I discovered *Famous Monsters, Spacemen, Creepy* and *Eerie*, those stories just poured out!'[14]

Untitled Play

In a phone interview prior to King's appearance at UMass Lowell in December 2012 he said, "The only play I'd written before *Ghost Brothers of Darkland County* was a play for my boy scout troupe when I was twelve and my relatives just absolutely adored it." This dates the play to between September 1959 and September 1960.

Queried for more information King responded[15]: "It was a one-acter. Guy lost in the woods finds this one house where the owner--an eccentric, for sure--takes him in. There's this steady pounding noise. The traveler finally asks, and the hermit tells him he's got the devil locked up in the cellar. "Boy," the traveler says (joking but nervous), "there's still a lot of bad stuff going on in the world, even though he IS locked up, right?" The hermit laughs. "Yes, but it would be so much worse if he was free, as he was until shortly after WWII--all those dead soldiers! All those dead Jews!" Anyway, I can't remember if the hermit guy left to do something or if he died, but the traveler was left alone, and he opened the door to let out the poor soul the hermit had taken prisoner. Only--surprise, except of course no one who ever watched THE TWILIGHT ZONE would be--it really WAS the devil. The only nice touch was that you never saw him. You just saw the traveler jerked into the dark...then screams...then fiendish laughter. "I'm FREE!" the devil cries as the stage goes dark. "Free to do my work in the world

[14] Personal correspondence with Rocky Wood, 18 December 2012
[15] Personal correspondence with Rocky Wood, 23 December 2012

again!" More fiendish laughter...the door starts to swing open... curtain. Remember, Rocky, I was only twelve, so cut me a break."

Updates to The Lost and Hidden Works

The following are updates to works *previously* surveyed in the *The Lost and Hidden Works* chapter. That chapter reviews the works of fiction that have never been seen by researchers and King experts, let alone fans. They have either been lost or King has held them so closely that they have not been read by anyone outside his inner circle. The search for 'lost' King work will continue unabated for decades. King himself still seeks the lost manuscript of *The Float*. The works covered here have either been completely lost; or it is known King holds them. Stories only 'rumored' to have been written or to exist are not surveyed.

I have been able to clarify some of the stories that have been mooted as by King with the master himself.

After the Play

After the Play was an epilogue to *The Shining* but was merged into the novel. King has stated the full version is lost. However, in 2013 an auction item was discovered, indicating the piece may actually be in the hands of an unknown collector. On September 23, 1993 Pacific Book Auction Galleries (Sale 29) auctioned "The Collection Formed by John McLaughlin of the Book Sail." One item offered, "Before The Play, 44 page typescript, plus the unpublished After (epilogue), a 4 page excerpt apparently from the manuscript of The Shining (numbered 517-520), all hand-corrected by King. Accompanied by a 2 page T.L.s/formal agreement from King's then-agent, Kirby McCauley, to Stuart David Schiff[16], signed by King, McCauley and Schiff. Binghampton, NY: Whispers Press, 1982 / This previously unpublished "prologue" to The Shining was cut from the published book by agreement between Doubleday & King, evidently because it would have added sufficient page count to add $1.00 to the retail cost of the book. This "prologue" was published by Stuart Schiff in the "Special Stephen King" issue of Whispers in 1982. The "After" segment is also signed by King,

---

[16] I checked with Schiff, who is certain he never saw the *After the Play* section of the manuscript

dated 10-13-84. Near Fine. (6000/8000)[17]" A separate chapter in *Stephen King: Unpublished, Uncollected* describes *Before the Play.*

Batman

This next piece had previously been reported as *Untitled* in the *Lost and Hidden Works* chapter but we now know its title to be *Batman.* The *Lisbon Monthly* for November 1986 carried an article titled *Stephen King: "Lisbon High's Most Celebrated Alumnus".*

In the piece Ambra Watkins reports King 'also wrote a successful script for Class Day about Batman and Robin.' More detail appears in the 1967 Lisbon High School Yearbook which reports, 'Two members of the Drum staff decided to write their own little skit for class night based on the television program, "Batman" ... Danny Emond and Steve King began writing their comic tale ... After finishing the script, the (senior class) committee approved the writing, made minor changes and began to put it together for the stage. Steve and Danny took the leading roles of Batman and Robin. The plot concerned a possible attack on Lisbon High which was to be prevented by the daring duo ... When Batman and Robin were needed, the two appeared on a tricycle down the middle of the gymnasium.' A photo from the yearbook shows King played Robin in the skit, performed on the evening of 7 June 1966. The class graduated the following day.

The full article in the High School Yearbook is headlined *Class Night Show Depicts "Batman"* and reads: 'Several weeks before the evening of June 7, 1966, members of the senior class of 1966 gathered with Mr. Aspinall to plan the class night ceremonies. Earlier in the year, the class night committee had planned to take movies of students during the winter and early spring and refer to them on the big evening. / Two members of the Drum[18] staff decided to write their own little skit for class night based on the television program, "Batman". After preliminary planning with Mr. Aspinall, Danny Emond and Steve King began writing their comic tale of Batman and Robin. After finishing the script, the committee approved the writing, made minor changes and began to put it together for the stage. Steve and Danny took the leading roles of Batman and Robin.

[17] Price estimate provided by the auction house
[18] The school newspaper

/ Pete Higgins and Tony Doyton portrayed Lisbon High's principal and his assistant. The plot concerned a possible attack on Lisbon High which was to be prevented by the daring duo, Batman and Robin. To introduce the program, out came Gloria Moore and Linda Bernier to do a bit of frugging, while Sandra Poulin gave a little speech to tell the audience just what was going on. / Members of the senior class portrayed students of Lisbon High. One of the funniest characters was played by Lewis Purinton. He was a problem student who was sent before the principal in his bermuda (*sic*) shorts, leather jacket, dark glasses, and carrying a beer bottle. / The plot thickened as the story of the class of 1966 poured forth. Memories of past years were made alive again amidst the thunder and lightning of a storm which raged outside. A few gifts were handed out to various seniors; several other seniors bequeathed various items to underclassmen. / When Batman and Robin were needed, the two appeared on a tricycle down the middle aisle of the gymnasium. After a few jumbled calls to one another, the two proceeded to the stage to assist the muddled administration. / At this point, the skit became an hilarious mixture of whodunit and antics of the two masked men. A bomb scare, a fight scene, and the entangling of Batman and Robin soon got everyone wondering what was going to happen next. / Finally, after all the annual business of class night had been taken care of – the awarding of gifts, the reading of the will, the class history reading, and the prediction of the future – and the little digs concerning school affairs had been made public – annual remarks on Strunkian English, class arguments and difficulties, and memories from the Washington trip – the class was ready to say a comic farewell to Lisbon High School. All the fun and games were held on this happy occasion before graduation. As far as the senior class of 1966 was concerned, their last contribution to the school had been made. Only the final legalities were left, that of graduation on June 8th. After removing the last of the grease paint, seniors left for parties and get-togethers and their last night as seniors.'

In April 2013 I enlisted the help of the Lisbon (Maine) Historical Society in searching for this piece. They discovered a partial typewritten script in their records – their long-serving Secretary, Dotty Smith deserves the credit for both preserving and rediscovering this amazing find. The play is titled *Batman* and the copy appears to have been donated by someone related to Peter Higgins (see above, Higgins played school principal 'Wiggins' in the play). In addition to the picture in the yearbook it is clear from the text that Stephen King played Robin and Danny Emond (who joined the US Navy shortly after graduation, served in Vietnam, and died in 1978[19]) took the role as Batman: "...Batman and Robin enter on the Batmobile, which is a decked-out tricycle. Batman is rather small, and Robin is on the back pushing." Emond is known to have been a small man and, of course, King is quite the opposite (particularly so for his age at the time).

I provided a copy of the script to King, who responded: "I can confirm that I wrote that damned high school skit. I recognize the type of my old Royal, which I eventually beat to death (the "n" went first, which I used in *Misery*). It's sort of embarrassing ..."[20] Of course, this piece is juvenilia and was intended as satire focused on their schoolmates as an audience. Most of us would find the same material from our school days equally embarrassing.

The partial script we have begins with Principal Wiggins (played by Pete Higgins, the son of the actual LHS Principal) learning from Mr Song (Tony Doyton) that the school duplicating machine and ten gallons of duplicating fluid had been stolen. A can of night crawlers (worms) was left in their place. Wiggins and Song immediately suspect the Creepy Crawler, who'd been digging huge holes all over the neighborhood and was extorting money from the rich, threatening to poison them with the night crawlers if they didn't pay up.

Wiggins calls Batman on the batphone and, while they wait for him to arrive, four students dance across the stage in a chorus-line routine. Three other students then attempt to explain the proceedings, including Batman's role in keeping Lisbon High free of crooks. First Speaker: "Why he single-handed cleaned up the Washington trip." The chorus-line reappears: "That's what you think!"

Batman (Danny Emond) and Robin (Stephen King) arrive in the Batmobile – 'a decked-out tricycle'. No sooner are they in conversation about the Creepy Crawler than there is a knock on the door. It's Lewis Corruptington (played by Lewis Purinton), a

---

[19] From research conducted by the Lisbon Historical Society in mid-April 2013
[20] Personal correspondence, 25 April 2013

'particularly odious student', accused of stealing bag lunches. He dressed in Bermuda shorts, a US drinking team sweatshirt, leather jacket and 'beatle boots'; and appeared to be drinking alcohol from a brown bottle (although he claims it is milk). Corruptington shows total disrespect for authority, Wiggins and the daring duo included. But, threatened with a large number of detentions, the miscreant offers a deal – information about the Creepy Crawler. Corruptington had found a desk filled with mud and night crawlers in a classroom, indicating the villain operated from the school premises.

Batman decides to send Robin undercover, as 'Ribbon Batsky'. Batman would observe Robin, masquerading as Leo Richer. Unfortunately that's where the partial script ends, without some of the action described in the Yearbook, such as the bomb scare, and fight scene. We must hope that another copy of the script exists somewhere and may yet come to light.

Ghost Brothers of Darkland County

This musical play has now been performed and King's libretto published. The premiere of this musical play was held at the Alliance Theatre, Atlanta, Georgia on 4 April 2012. King's libretto appears in a book (which also includes printed song lyrics, a cast CD recording and some material on DVD) – *Ghost Brothers of Darkland County* by Stephen King, John Mellencamp and T-Bone Burnett (Concord Music Group, 2013).

In addition to the libretto King wrote the lyrics for the song *So Goddam Good*. The credit in the book reads, "So Goddam Good" by John Mellencamp, T Bone Burnett and Stephen King[21] and the lyrics appear on pages 82 and 83.

The Pit and the Pendulum

King wrote *The Pit and the Pendulum*, which he and Chris Chesley sold copies of at Durham's elementary school. It 'novelized' the 1961 movie of the same name. All trace of the story has been lost. King tells its story ('...turned out to be my first best-seller') in section 18 of the *C.V.* part of *On Writing*. King's entertaining re-telling of the whole incident, in which he also reveals selling

[21] King confirmed he wrote the lyrics in an email to Rocky Wood, 23 October 2013

copies of another story, *The Invasion of the Star-Creatures* that summer, is highly recommended. Concluding his retelling of the incident King says, 'Miss Hisler told me I would have to give everyone's money back. I did so with no argument, even to those kids (and there were quite a few, I'm happy to say) who insisted on keeping their copies of V.I.B. #1. I ended up losing money on the deal after all, but when summer vacation came I printed four dozen copies of a new story, an original called *The Invasion of the Star-Creatures*[22], and sold all but four or five.' Note that some kids 'insisted on keeping their copies' of this story. Unlikely though it may seem, is it possible a copy will turn up one day when one of King's ex-schoolmates cleans out an old box of keepsakes?

King had previously related the history *The Pit and the Pendulum* in Douglas Winter's *The Art of Darkness*.[23] 'One day I went to Brunswick to see the American International Film of *The Pit and the Pendulum* with Vincent Price, and I was very impressed by it – very, very scared. And when I went home, I got a bunch of stencils, and I wrote a novelization of the movie, with chapters and everything – although it was only twelve pages long. I bought a ream of typewriter paper, and I bought a stapler and some staples, and I printed, on Dave's machine, about two hundred and fifty copies of this book. I slugged in a price of a dime on them, and when I took them to school, I was just flabbergasted. In three days, I sold something like seventy of these things. And all of a sudden, I was in the black – it was like a license to steal. That was my first experience with bestsellerdom. But they shut me down. They took me to the principal's office and told me to stop, although there didn't seem to be any real reason. My aunt[24] taught in that school, and it was just not seemly; it wasn't right. So I had to quit.'

Further information about this tale came to light in late 2012 when an item offered on eBay turned to out to a be a one page flyer King had created to advertise stories from his cottage publishing

---

[22] In November 2011 King confirmed to Rocky Wood in personal correspondence that this is actually the same story as *The Star Invaders*. That story is subject of a separate chapter in *Stephen King: Unpublished, Uncollected*.

[23] Stephen King: *The Art of Darkness*, Douglas E Winter, p.19

[24] Ethelyn Flaws, husband of Oren (both are referred to in *Song of Susannah*), sister of Ruth Pillsbury King

venture, Triad Publishing Ltd. This was the name King used to publish *People, Places and Things* (1960 and 1963) and *The Star Invaders* (June 1964). The flyer was posted to a fellow fan in New York and is postmarked 5pm, 6 September 1963 at the Pownal, Maine Post Office. It advertises three stories for sale – *The Pit and the Pendulum, Trigger-Finger* and *The Undead*. Offered for sale for 20¢ the description for *The Pit and the Pendulum* read: 'this is NOT Poe's classic. It's adapted from the A-I shocker, starring Vincent Price. What's it about? Torture...premature burial...and the shambling horror that walked the darkened corridors of the storm-ravaged castle!'

Untitled

In an interview in *Twilight Zone* magazine for April 1981, King said: 'Yes, among the stories I submitted to *Cavalier* was one I thought had a really nice twist. It's about a vampire that's a coal miner - so he can more or less be on the job all the time, since he's underground where it's always dark. There's a cave-in, and this vampire drinks all his mates blood while they wait for the others to dig them out. Of course, when he goes out into the sun, he sort of evaporates.' However, when I queried this with King he replied, 'I remember that one well. It was never written, but maybe someday it will be. Thus, the less said, the better.'[25]

Untitled

In an interview with *Gallery* magazine for January 1986 King had this to say: 'I worry about airplanes. I can remember being on a transcontinental flight and getting to the halfway point - which the stewardesses always announce with great cheer - although what they are actually saying is that you are now too far to turn back. You either have to go ahead or die. And I thought, what if somebody said, "I need a pillow," and the stewardess opened the overhead rack and all these rats came out into her face and she started to scream, and the rats were biting off her nose and everything else, and one of the people in first class opened up a pouch to get an air-sick bag because this was so gross, and rats came out of there, rats came out of everywhere. And the name of this story was going to be "The Rats Are Loose on

[25] Personal correspondence, 14 January 2013

Flight 74." I just haven't got around to writing it yet, but I probably will.' King confirmed to me he never actually wrote the story.[26]

Untitled

Update to this entry: According to Chris Chesley, there was another such story, although he does provide the title. Chesley told Beahm[27], 'In another story, King playfully wove fact and fiction, using the real names of fellow students in a fictional hostage situation. "It was all of twenty pages," recalled Chesley, "and it was a story where he used real kids who had taken over the grammar school. Of course, the people that were in the story read the story; because of things like that, King was lionized. He could take real people and set them into this setting where we were heroes. In this story, we died fighting the National Guard. The kids he liked best 'died' last; so naturally, we were all wondering when we were going to 'die'."

When I asked King about this tale he responded: 'Sure, I remember that story; I must have been in the fifth grade at the time. Today I probably would have been arrested as a potential terrorist, but it was just for fun, a way to pass the time when we were all bored. If it had a title, I don't remember it.'[28] This dates it to circa 1957/58.

Update to Further Notes

It has also been speculated that King wrote *New Blood* by Richard Salem (McDonald Futura 1981 and Signet, 1982). King confirmed he did not write this novel[29].

Update to The Uncollected, and the Unpublished section

This section updates material in *The Uncollected, and the Unpublished* section of the Fourth Edition of *Stephen King: Uncollected, Unpublished.*

The Glass Floor

The Glass Floor was reprinted in *Cemetery Dance* magazine (issue #68, 2012), along with King's *Introduction* from the Fall

[26] Personal correspondence, 5 January 2013
[27] *The Stephen King Story*, George Beahm, p.26
[28] Personal correspondence with Rocky Wood, 23 August 2013
[29] Personal correspondence with Rocky Wood, 1 February 2013

1990 *Weird Tales* issue. Back issues are easy to obtain from www.cemeterydance.com.

The Leprechaun

In 1987 King attempted and abandoned *Phil and Sundance* (see separate section following), which seems to be a working out of the same story-line as *The Leprechaun*.

Maximum Overdrive

Asked on 7 December 2012 at UMass Lowell if Dysart's Truck Stop (actually Dysart's Truck Stop & Restaurant) in Bangor, Maine was an inspiration for *Maximum Overdrive*, King confirmed it was.

People, Places and Things

King owns the sole known copy of the collection, which he re-discovered in his papers in 1985. However, partial photocopies of the 'Second Printing, 1963' version circulate freely in the King community. It is thought that less than a dozen original copies were ever printed.[30] In 2013 King confirmed he wrote the 'Forward' (*sic*): 'I wrote it. It was only a paragraph or so, kind of a *Twilight Zone* lead-in.'[31]

The Poems - Update to The Dark Man

The Dark Man (1969)

This poem was first published in the University of Maine literary publication *Ubris* for Fall 1969 and was reprinted without changes in a small magazine, *Moth*, in 1970 (in both publications the poem is credited as 'Steve King'), along with two other King poems. Its next publication was not until *The Devil's Wine*, nearly three and a half decades later, in 2004. This may be explained by the fact that this poem serves as the basis for one of King's most significant characters, Randall Flagg, the anti-hero of *The Stand* and a key opponent for Roland in *The Dark Tower* Cycle. In 2013 King allowed the short poem *The Dark Man* to be published by Cemetery Dance in a mass market form for the first time, in *The Dark Man: An Illustrated Poem*, with

---

[30] According to Chesley, in George Beahm's *The Stephen King Story*
[31] Personal correspondence with Rocky Wood, 14 August 2013

the illustrations of Glenn Chadbourne the centerpiece – after all the poem is two pages long, and there are over 70 pages of illustration!

The Plant

In 2000 King updated the first version of *The Plant* – the original version was published by King's Philtrum Press as a signed, Limited Edition and provided as a Christmas gift from the Kings in 1982, 1983 and 1985. The new version was released on the Internet via his official website, www.stephenking.com. This followed the phenomenal success of his serial novel *The Green Mile* (at one point it held six places of the top ten on *The New York Times* bestseller list) and of *Riding the Bullet*. After the latter was released on the Internet on 14 March 2000 it was quickly downloaded more than half a million times! Both these successes prompted King to try *The Plant* as a subscription based offering on the 'Net.

After six parts *The Plant* folded its leaves again, with the story still unfinished. The first five parts, issued from July through November 2000, were charged on an 'honor' system, where the buyers downloaded the text and were expected to send in their payment. The last part was given away from 4 December by King as a Christmas gift to his readers and, presumably, as a small apology for stopping the story mid-stream, again! King also announced the six installments had formed the first part of the novel, with that part to be known as *Zenith Rising*.

All six parts were once available for download for $7.00 but are now free at http://www.stephenking.com/library/novel/plant:_zenith _rising_the.html[32].

Something Wicked This Way Comes screenplay

The first three paragraphs are revised to read:

The screenplay of *Something Wicked This Way Comes* is held in Box 1010 at the Special Collections Unit of the Raymond H Fogler Library at the University of Maine, Orono. Written permission from King is required to access this work.

In an interview with David Chute (published in *Take One* for

---

[32] As of March 2014

January 1979 and reproduced in *Feast of Fear*[33]) King talks of having written this script, saying: "...I felt more divorced from the source material. I loved the book, and I think that of all the screenplays I've done, that was the best. But in spite of loving it I was a little divorced from it, where I wasn't with my own book."

On 7 December 2012 King told students at UMass Lowell this was the first screenplay he ever wrote. He wrote it as practice and to see what it was like to write in that form, "I'd been writing novels full time for about a year and a half and I thought to myself I want to learn how to write movies. I want to try it anyway, so I got a book – it was about writing screenplays and I read it and it was bullshit. But at the end it had a sample screenplay from *The Twilight Zone*. It showed me what the form was and that wasn't bullshit, that was something real that I could ... so I took the Ray Bradbury book *Something Wicked This Way Comes* and I wrote a screenplay and I learned what I was doing – it wasn't for anybody but me. And a little while later I wrote a book called *The Shining*." King retired from teaching and took up full-time writing in May/June 1973 and dated a manuscript of *The Shining* on 16 December 1974. From this we can glean that the *Something Wicked This Way Comes* screenplay was written in 1974.

The Stand Screenplays - Update to Unproduced Movie Screenplay

Considering the varying timelines for the different versions of *The Stand* it is interesting that King chose to set this particular script in 1985 (the superflu outbreak begins in Arnette on 16 June 1985 and the nuclear explosion in Las Vegas occurs on 5 November 1985). Various sources note that King began writing scripts for a movie version of *The Stand* as early as 1979. In an interview for *Starburst* magazine (#54, 1982), King said, 'George optioned *The Stand* which is a very long novel. I've done a couple of drafts and I've still got a screenplay that's the size of The Bible.' And, in an interview for denofgeek.com (the interview was conducted in 1983 but posted on the website in 2007) King confirmed the screenplay was for George Romero. So, in 1983 he said, 'I've

---

[33] Feast of Fear: *Conversations with Stephen King*, Tim Underwood and Chuck Miller (editors), page 79

done two drafts of the screenplay ... and I'm gonna go back this summer and do a third draft.' This properly dates the screenplay.

Stories from Journals - Update to *The Evaluation*

This is a part manuscript only. There are twelve single pages. The notation heading it in King's handwriting reads 'The Evaluation'.

In this America Under Siege tale a psychologist, Dr. Peter Judkins, prepared to evaluate Edgar Roos at the Crown County Mental Hospital in New York. Roos had been arrested after killing nine people that day, two with a butcher's knife and seven with a shotgun. The murderer had left his will in a locker.

Initially uncommunicative and sitting strait-jacketed and chained to an oak chair that was bolted to the floor, Roos told Judkins he might talk if Judkins took off a Band-Aid covering a shaving cut! The fragment ends at this point.

Edgar Roos was a slender young man, weighing about 150 pounds. He had a narrow face, glossy black hair and wore glasses. The killings had earned him the nickname 'The Commuter Killer'. All we really know of Dr. Judkins was that he had been married for eleven years. There is only one other character of note, a technician wearing an orderly's uniform, Hector Alonzo. He was to video and audiotape the interview and had also provided Dr. Judkins with the key to the locker in which Roos had left his will.

Judkins was assigned to evaluate Roos because the psychologist on call that week, Livermore, had just had his gall bladder removed (we are left with the uneasy impression that this might turn out to be bad luck for Judkins, and good luck for Livermore). Seven other psychologists were affiliated with the Crown County Mental Hospital.

The Crown County Mental Hospital is in 'the smallest county in the State of New York'. There is also a Crown City in the County (confused yet?) and the Crown City High School and Crown City YMCA are mentioned.

A magazine article from September 1990 in which King discusses this story was brought to my attention in 2013[34]: It's the dance again, the art of skipping along the precipice without falling in. And you

---

[34] 'Stephen King Scares Himself' in 'Image' (a supplement to San Francisco, California newspaper, *The Examiner*), pages 8ff

do it by telling stories, says King, stories with "one little thing" – the innocent thing with a twist of evil that defines the *danse macabre.* / So now there's this story he wants to write "about this guy who's a shrink in maybe upstate New York. His job is to evaluate people who've been brought in by the police for one thing or another, and he has an interview with this guy who's this mass murderer. That day, he's killed seven or eight people, and he's been captured. And he sits down with the shrink, and he's wearing leg irons and everything and he says to the shrink, 'I see that, uh, you've got a Band-Aid on your neck. What's that for?' And the shrink says, 'Well I cut myself shaving. Let's talk about you.' And the guy says, 'No, let's talk about the Band-Aid. I'll talk to you if you'll take the Band-Aid off and show me that you really did cut yourself shaving.' So the shrink, who's used to odd requests from crazy people, takes the Band-Aid off, and sure enough there's a little scab on it, and the guy says, 'OK. I did it because I found out that almost everybody in the world isn't real. They're just stuffed people. They're just, like, teddy bears. All they are is dressing for these awful Masters that run everything.' And the shrink says, 'Well, that's very interesting,' and sends the guy away." / King's voice drops to a whisper. "Then, when he's left alone in his office, he takes the Band-Aid off again. He scrapes off a little bit of makeup and pushes in just a tiny bit of stuffing. And he puts the Band-Aid back on. / "It's just that one little thing, but I think it would work," says King. "It's those little off-kilter things ..."

Typical of King, the story is already fascinating by the time it stops abruptly after only a few pages. It seems unlikely that King will again pick up this particular storyline, but it would seem certain that the reader would be in for not a few chills, spills and twists if he did!

Weeds

Weeds was originally published in *Cavalier* (a men's magazine) for May 1976 and reprinted in *Nugget* (another men's magazine) for April 1979. In *Cavalier* the story is listed in the Index as *Weeds* but the headline to the story, spread over two pages, reads: 'More Than a Green Thumb ... Will Be Necessary to Stop the Weeds: A chilling new story by the author of *Carrie* and *'Salem's Lot.'* When questioned about the title in 2012 King replied, "That "more than a green thumb" stuff went above the title. It was a come-on."[35] This confirms the title as simply *Weeds*.

It has never been reproduced in text format in a King collection and it is far from clear why. It is certainly a far better story than some of the 'pulp' fiction stories that King did allow into his collections, such as *Night Shift*, published in 1978. King clearly has a fond spot for the story itself but perhaps as the years passed found the text version less and less capable of meeting the tone set for each of his short story collections? Alternately, perhaps after *Creepshow* was released in 1982 King no longer felt a need to republish?

Whatever the answer to why it had not been collected, King relented to a degree, agreeing to allow *Weeds* to be reprinted in *Shivers VII*, an anthology edited by Richard Chizmar and released by Cemetery Dance in 2013.

New Unpublished Stories:
Mr Mercedes

This novel, due for publication on 3 June 2014, first came to public attention when King mentioned the manuscript and title while talking to students at the University of Massachusetts in Lowell, Massachusetts on 7 December 2012. According to a press report[36]: 'Many of his best book ideas occur come to him as mutated observations of real-life happenings, King explained, including a recently completed 500-page manuscript that focuses on a suicidal police officer six months into his retirement, who receives a letter from a gloating killer. "I wanted to write it as a short story, and end it with the cop putting the gun in his mouth. But now, instead of a 12-page short story, I've got a 500-page manuscript -- because the thing just grew."

From the publisher: 'Following the phenomenal success of DOCTOR SLEEP, a No. 1 international hardback bestseller, Stephen King has written a riveting cat-and-mouse suspense thriller about a retired cop and a couple of unlikely allies who race against time to stop a lone killer intent on blowing up thousands. / Retired homicide detective Bill Hodges is haunted by the few cases he left open, and by one in particular: in the pre-dawn hours, hundreds of desperate unemployed people were lined up for a spot at a job fair in a distressed

---

[35] Personal correspondence with King, 22 April 2012
[36] At www.lowellsun.com

Midwestern city. Without warning, a lone driver ploughed through the crowd in a stolen Mercedes. Eight people were killed, fifteen wounded. The killer escaped. / Months later, on the other side of the city, Bill Hodges gets a letter in the mail, from a man claiming to be the perpetrator. He taunts Hodges with the notion that he will strike again. Hodges wakes up from his depressed and vacant retirement, hell-bent on preventing that from happening. / Brady Hartfield lives with his alcoholic mother in the house where he was born. And he is indeed preparing to kill again. / Hodges, with a couple of misfit friends, must apprehend the killer in this high-stakes race against time because Brady's next mission, if it succeeds, will kill or maim hundreds, even thousands. / Mr Mercedes is a war between good and evil, from the master of suspense whose insight into the mind of this obsessed, insane killer is chilling and unforgettable.'

Phil and Sundance

In April 2013 a man tried to sell what he said was an 82 page manuscript for a "novella that SK wrote about 1987". He claimed he came to own the manuscript for *Phil and Sundance* because he "was the lucky recipient of a make-a-wish foundation wish to meet Stephen King when I was thirteen years old." He also published a scan of the first page. When queried King responded, "It's legit, all right, but it's hazy--All I remember is that it was about little people..."[37]

The scanned page starts Chapter One – 'Phil and the Thing on the Stairs' and we immediately discover it is a Derry story (Phil is attending Mary Deere Elementary, which is not mentioned elsewhere in King's fiction). We learn that Phil is ten and 'big' – a few kids call him 'Fatso' but, because he is likeable, most kids just called him by his name. Phil does not like broccoli, phys ed, the thirteen year old kid from across the street who had once beaten him up, or a certain breed of birds: "He didn't like crows[38]. Bad luck. You poked the sign of the evil eye at them – his dad had taught him that ..."

After some 'negotiations' the manuscript was purchased by one of King's publishers – Cemetery Dance. King then authorized a copy be released to me for review in this book. Later, his personal assistant

[37] Personal correspondence with Rocky Wood, 18 April 2013
[38] In an interview with *The New York Times Magazine* King's son Joe said of his father: "ravens freak him out, crows freak him out a little bit ..."

posted this at the official website's message board: "I'm glad to hear Cemetery Dance was the one to obtain it as we trust them to do the right thing. I've known about the manuscript for quite some time as we have a copy in our files although we don't have the complete manuscript – ours end at page 101 but it is mid-sentence although there are other unnumbered pages that may continue it." So, there are clearly two versions in existence. However, it is very unlikely King will ever complete the work. The review below is from the 82 page manuscript.

Chapter One – 'Phil and the Thing on the Stairs'. We learn that Phil Wentworth (who lives in Derry) is home sick, one of a long list of things he doesn't like. He is ten, tall for his age, overweight and attends Mary Deere Elementary. He thinks himself a coward and, when he hears creaks on the stairs, imagines a killer is coming for him – only to find it's his sister's Siamese cat, Bill. We learn a little about Phil's parents (his father works at McCracken Ford, owned by the father of Phil's thirteen year old bully neighbor; and his mother works at Derry Business Machines – his dad is superstitious and both parents have many favorite sayings, which Phil calls 'weirdisms').

Chapter Two – Bill and Sundance. We learn that Phil likes a lot of things too, but like all big kids most of these were not good for him, particularly fast food and pizza. He liked watching TV, staying up late and Big-Time Wrestling, even though his father said it was fake. He liked tacos, which made him fart, which in turn irritated his older sister, Dina (who was 14 or 15). Among the things he liked some were good for him: 'Although he was cautious about who had (*sic*) admitted it to (some people would laugh and say you were a pantywaist), he liked school, especially math and geography.' He also liked Song and Dance Interpretation, although the square dance unit had proved he was a nerd – 'a beefy sonofagun who had to alamand (*sic*) left and dosy-do right with a partner who was three inches shorter and sixty pounds lighter than you.'

Phil awoke from a nightmare by falling out of bed. Realizing he had slept for a while he decided to check the time, 'And that's when the weird stuff *really* started.' The clock was by the window and, looking out, he saw Bill (the Siamese cat), 'murdering Sundance'. Sundance turns out to be a 'Teeny', 'barely six inches high', a miniature humanoid from a species 'nearing extinction' from the depredations of 'Bigs', particularly birds. 'The tribe' to which he belonged was desperate – suffering from a recurring cycle of disease ('The Spots') and a bad harvest, their Council had decided on a 'Lone Foray' - a member sent 'for the food and herbs they so badly needed.' Sundance was the third to draw a lot for the Lone Foray – the young man and young woman before had never returned. Sundance had found food and herbs and was dragging them on the sledge back to 'the Den' when the cat struck.

Delving into Bill's mind we find he is astonished to find he's stalking a *Teeny*. 'Hard to believe but absolutely true. Of course he had heard the birds talking, saying there was a tribe of them somewhere about, but Bill put little stock in what birds said, even fairly intelligent ones like robins ... Bogie, his grandfather, had told him a great deal about Teenies once, a long time ago, when Bill was just a kit. Bogie had said that once there had been a great many Teenies in the world, and that it was a pity they were getting so thin ... No cat ate anything better than a Teeny.' We learn that Siamese think of 'Humes' as their pets and go to great lengths to conceal their true nature as killers and appear amenable, all the better to 'train' or 'domesticate' us! We get an insight into the secret world of pets – for instance Persians thought of mixed breed cats scornfully as 'Hash Cats'; that the cat equivalent of the Humes' Bogeyman was 'Dripslobber, the supposed Queen of the Dogs'. When Bill had enquired of his grandfather at the pet shop where he was born and sold to the Wentworth family, if Teenies were 'Leper-Cons', Bogie denied it: "That story was made up by dogs, and passed on, I'm sorry to say, by cats almost as stupid as they are ... The word is even wrong ... The right one is Leprechauns. Leprechauns are small creatures – creatures, not Humes or animals – that are supposed to live on the other side of the big water the Humes call the Ocean." Amongst the rumors Bogie had heard about Leprechauns is that "Old Man Splitfoot lets the leprechauns live forever if they will steal a Hume baby and replace it with a troll-baby ..." Bogie goes on to tell Bill if he ever comes across a Teeny to kill it quick as they can be dangerous when cornered.

When Bill first leapt at Sundance his claws raked two 'deep gores' in his back but missed the killing stroke. When he pounced again, he came up short, 'as Sundance's spear struck deep in the pad of one claw.' Bill attacked again, breaking the spear, and now relaxed and began to swing his clawed paw in the coup de grace.

Chapter Three: Phil and Sundance. Phil is like most young boys – he has doubts but he generally likes himself. However, he is reminded of one of his not so good moments – when he came up in a Little League game with the scores tied, one on and one out and hit into a double play. Worse, the opponent was McCracken Ford and his nemesis Dell McCracken was at first base. And of other times he'd not come up to snuff – backing out of riding Space Mountain, still not being able to ride a bicycle and being afraid to ride in his father's old Convertible Mustang – in case 'the brakes failed on Kansas Street, or on Main Street – both hills were steep enough so that there would probably be just enough left of them to bury. / In cigar boxes.' Overall, despite being overweight Phil 'was cheerful most of the time.' But, 'When you got right down to it, the worst thing of all was Dell McCracken.' Both Phil and his sister realized they could do nothing about Dell's bullying, 'because something might happen to their Dad's job' at McCracken Ford: 'John Wentworth had worked his way up from just another of McCracken's Mechanics to Department Head, and although he was making good money, he still called Mr. McCracken Simon Legree, which meant he still felt like a slave.'

All Phil's fears were swept aside as he saw the cat attacking something in the grass –something that looked like a little person. (Here, King foreshadows a part of the story we will never read: Phil 'was afraid later, yeah, he spent three weeks in constant terror as one thing after another happened like a string of firecrackers going off ...') As Phil ran downstairs, Bill prepared the killing stroke of his claws but realized that he would take little man's head off, which just wouldn't do - 'Bill was extremely fond of brains ... Siamese cats and Hash Cats shared this one idea (and only this, other than their belief in the great Cat-God Anubis, which all cats share); the reason brains taste so good is because they are good for you. The smarter the brain you eat the smarter you become. And if this really was a miniature Hume, he would be doing his own mind a dreadful disservice to waste good brains ...' As a result Bill's blow merely raked the Small's face ('they would heal to thin, grim lines of white scar that Sundance would wear to the end of his days.') Sundance took the opportunity to dart forward and grab on to the cat's lower chest, which made Bill furious: 'You have to understand this ... the reason other animals regard Humes and Siamese with more fear and caution than they do any others ... is because ... they are the only animals that sometimes go mad.' When Phil yelled at the cat to stop, it entered that very state of temporary insanity – trying to shake off and kill the Teeny and then attacking Phil ('Fill' in Bill's thoughts) when he made the mistake of grabbing the feline. Bill bit Phil's palm and raked his arm with his claws, while Sundance was flung away into the grass. Sundance turned to help his erstwhile savior, his broken spear in hand, and called to both cat and boy. Phil brought his arm down to the Teeny's level and Sundance stabbed the cat 'where Bill's tail joined his back', forcing him to release claws and teeth as Phil swung his arm – the attacker landed twenty feet away but headed straight back to the fray. Phil picked Sundance up and kicked the oncoming cat 'in the chest as hard as he could'.

The kick had cleared Bill's madness but he sent a thought to Phil: "Tell him ... that I'm going to kill him. That's a promise. It's only a question of when ..." But Sundance had passed out or, Phil feared when he looked at the bloody body in his hands, worse: 'He looked dead.' What would he, what could he, do now: 'Phil realized he was on his own.'

Chapter Four: Phil on His Own. Phil had taken the Teeny into the kitchen, where his loose pajama pants fell down - he absently stepped out of them, only the pain in his arm keeping him from totally zoning out. He remembered his father's dictum about mechanics – 'Step by Step' and focused on the problem. How much time did he have until his mother came home – that was step one. It was 4.50pm, which probably left him no more than twenty five minutes. 'Step Two: Find out if the tiny guy was still alive.' Regarding the limp body Phil was pretty sure he wasn't a leprechaun – they were 'supposed to have pointed ears, green blood, and speak in Irish accents ...'

Phil remembered his Poppa's funeral – when he thought he could see the dead man's chest rising and falling. When he raised this with his mother she opined that was because he wanted his grandfather to be alive. Phil said that wasn't it: 'All of a sudden, Phil thought he knew why kids had to turn into grown-ups. It was because if you stayed a kid forever, the grown-ups would eventually drive you crazy with their stupid ideas and their deaf ears. He guessed that in the end you turned into a grown-up in simple self-defense.' Phil's Uncle Jerry, a teacher, intervened saying that he too had seen the shallow rise and fall of the dead man's chest but also explaining that it was an hallucination ("Or maybe 'optical illusion' is the correct term") caused by the brain, which never having seen a familiar person lifeless before, simply inserts the illusion of breathing into one's brain.

That lesson had Phil convinced that just 'seeing' shallow breathing from the Teeny did not mean it was alive – he'd need more proof. 'He suddenly had an idea. A good one ...' and ran to get a mirror from his mother's vanity case. When he held the mirror to the little man's face it misted, just a little. Panicking as to what to do next, Phil flicked cold water on the Teeny and started to ask him what to do, dropping his voice to a whisper so as not to hurt him further. 'The little man's eyes fluttered open, and Phil stopped speaking. In truth, he wasn't sure he could have spoken if his life depended on (sic). The small man's eyes were dark ... dark with shock, dark with pain. / Dark he was ... and golden-eyed.'

When the Teeny tried to talk Phil couldn't hear him, so he rolled up a piece of sheet music to form a tube, through which he could faintly discern what was being said. Sundance managed to explain he had been pulling a sledge and he needed something orange from it before fainting. Phil ran for the door and was searching the sledge when the realized he had pulled off a 'totally humungous screw-up ... He had come running out so fast he had forgotten to put on his pajama bottoms again. Except for the bloody dish-towel wrapped around his right arm the kid was bucky-tailed naked.' Worse, he heard the klaxon from Dell McCracken's bike, Dell riding with his brother ('that little scab Sonny') on the handlebars – they hadn't seen him yet but would soon enough. 'Phil froze,' and his mind now told him to run for it, little guy or not – 'The kid booked it for the house, empty-handed.'

'Except for good or ill, that wasn't how it happened, except in the part of Phil's mind that really was as yellow as the stripe up the main highway ... He jerked convulsively, and then went on looking at the stuff in the little man's sledge.' He saw something bright orange and then heard the dreaded Dell McCracken call out, "*Heyyyyyyyyyyyyyyyy, Nature Boy!*" 'He tried to yell something else, but couldn't do it. He was laughing hysterically.' Despite the distraction Phil gathered up shreds of an orange, carrot-like material.

And there the chapter and manuscript ends.

But not our investigation. *Phil and Sundance* is clearly another attempt at the story-line King was working on in *The Leprechaun*, which has been dated to around 1983, four years earlier. In that story (see *The Leprechaun* chapter in *Stephen King: Uncollected, Unpublished*) it is Owen King who interrupts his sister's cat (this time named Springsteen) tormenting something on the lawn, a '...*person*, a tiny little man wearing a green hat made out of a leaf. The little man looked back over his shoulder, and Owen saw how scared the little guy was.'

The struggle between a little man-like creature and a cat forms the basis of the screenplay *General* and a segment of the related movie script *Cat's Eye*, although the roles are reversed in that tale, with the cat being the hero. Those pieces were written around 1984, before King attempted and abandoned *Phil and Sundance*.

There are a number of links in the manuscript to King's other fiction. With a Derry setting this unpublished fragment is linked to other Derry tales. Derry also appears in *Autopsy Room Four, Bag of Bones, The Bird and the Album, 11/22/63, Insomnia, It, The Road Virus Heads North (999), The Road Virus Heads North (Everything's Eventual)* and *Secret Window, Secret Garden*. It receives considerable mention in *Dreamcatcher* and *The Tommyknockers*. It is also mentioned in *The Body, Comb Dump, The Dark Half, The Dark Tower VII: The Dark Tower, Dolores Claiborne, Gerald's Game, Hearts in Atlantis, Mrs. Todd's Shortcut, Pet Sematary, The Revelations of 'Becka Paulson, The Running Man, Storm of the Century, Uncle Otto's Truck (Skeleton Crew)* and *Uncle Otto's Truck (Yankee)*.

In Chapter One we learn that 'Dell McCracken is thirteen and would be going to high school when summer vacation is over.' The high school is named in Chapter Two as 'Derry High', which appears in *Dreamcatcher* and *Insomnia*. '...the Mall' is mentioned in Chapter One, the only other mentions of a Mall in Derry being in *Bag of Bones*; as well as the Derry Mall in *The Tommyknockers* and *It*. In Chapter Two Phil's Song and Dance Interpretation Class went on a field trip to see *Peter and the Wolf* at 'Bangor High'. In

The Dark Tower VI: Song of Susannah we learn that Owen King graduated from Bangor High. The Wentworths and the McCrackens lived on Jackson Street, Derry, which also appears in *Bag of Bones, Insomnia* and *It*. Kansas Street, Derry is mentioned and also appears in *Secret Window, Secret Garden, Dreamcatcher, Insomnia, It* and both versions of *The Road Virus Heads North*. Main Street, Derry is mentioned and also appears in *Insomnia, It* and *The Tommyknockers*.

Revival

In an interview to support the Mark Twain House on 18 July 2013 King revealed some details about a book he was writing called *Revival*: "The main character is a kid who learns to play guitar, and I could relate to this guy because he's not terribly good. But he's just good enough to catch on with a couple of bands to play for a lot of years and the song he learns to play first is the song I learned to play first, *Cherry, Cherry* by Neal Diamond." This novel will be published on 11 November 2014.

Untitled

In October 2013 King sent me some holographic material in the form of two legal pads, each about half full of his writing and notes; and some loose sheets. One pad can be easily dated to 2002 as it contains first draft material from *The Dark Tower VII: The Dark Tower* and a box score from the Boston Red Sox – Cleveland Indians game on June 25 that year. The second pad appears to be from 2012 or 2013. The loose sheets include draft material and notes for *11/22/63, Cell* and *Doctor Sleep*.

Fascinating as all that material was the real treasure was two and a bit pages from an unknown story. When I asked King if he recalled anything about what looked like a busted tale he replied, 'The story is mine, but I don't remember it. The "oral narrative" doesn't seem to work, so I guess that's why I ditched it.'[39]

The piece has a typically compelling opening: 'Don't tell me the dead don't come back cause I know better. And that's all I'm gonna say about it. The rest is what I seen and a very little I didn't. But when I guess at a thing I will tell you.' The narrator, whose first

[39] Email from King, 29 December 2013

name we never learn (his surname is Donovan) relates that he and his mother had come to live with his dead father's brother, 'Uncle Son' on a farm in Tennessee. Although his dying father had said the uncle was 'bound to give her $500' ... 'from the farm.', when she rang he only offered to take them in and put them to work. 'She didn't mention the $500 then because we didn't have nowhere else to go.' The mother added: 'I knowed there wasn't no five hundred dollars just from the sound of his voice ... but I couldn't bear to hear him say it.' When the narrator left the house after kissing his father moments before he passed, 'There I seen a redbird perched on the handle of the plow and it came to me that the hand of some other boy's Pa would be on it before a week was out, because even in Georgia God's season is short and everyone knows crops won't wait.'

The handwritten text includes an eerie echo of *Dolan's Cadillac*. A hearse came for his father's body: 'That funeary was pretty fine, a Cadillac with whitewall tires, and so at least one Donovan got to ride in a Cadillac.' Note: the spelling is 'funeary' not 'funerary'.

Neighbors gave them $5 to travel to Tennessee, but the money ran out 60 miles short of the town of Budd, where Uncle Son lived. A man they hitched a ride with gave his mother $5 more, but only after taking her behind some bushes at a picnic spot. 'I ast her why he had to take her in the bushes to give her that money and she said it was because some people were ashamed of their own generosity. I didn't understand her then, but now I'm two years older and know more than I did. More than I want to, at least about some things.' And there the story fragment ends.

Yet again we see the ease in which King establishes a tale, with interesting characters whose story appeals.

Untitled – *Under the Dome* episode

In February 2014 King confirmed to me[40] that he had written the first episode of the TV series *Under the Dome*'s Season 2. It is extremely unlikely this will ever be published but readers will be able to view the episode on DVD.

---

[40] Personal correspondence with King, 28 February 2014

New Published but Uncollected Stories:
A Face in the Crowd

This story is a collaboration between King and Stuart O'Nan; they previously collaborated on the non-fiction volume, *Faithful* (2004). Both are baseball related. It was first published on 21 August 2012 in varying eBook formats and as an audio book, so is easily obtained.

The focus of this lengthy story is a widower – a transplanted New Englander living on the Gulf Coast of Florida, a Red Sox fan who'd coached Little League and had 'magnanimously adopted the Devil Rays ... as his second team.' Not unlike Stephen King himself (although he only winters in Florida). Dean Evers had been married for forty six years and understands that watching the Rays on TV most nights was 'just a way of passing time' after his wife's death.

One night Evers sees his old childhood dentist sitting in the Ray's home crowd. The sight stuns Evers – he hasn't seen the man in over fifty years but he doesn't appear to have aged and is dressed in his 'white sanitary smock'. He rationalizes the man must be a strikingly similar relative of the dentist. Later in the game, when Evers checks the seat behind home plate the man had been sitting in, it's empty and remains that way. In bed, still awake at 3am, he worries that seeing Dr. Young might be a sign or an omen of some sort.

The next night he tunes in again. Late in the game he spots 'three rows deep, in the same pinstripe suit he was buried in, his old business partner Leonard Wheeler.' Evers and Wheeler had created a successful truck rental business but the relationship had soured over the business' direction and Wheeler's overbearing manner. Evers keeps his eyes glued to the TV; when the camera returns to Wheeler's seat it is just as empty as Dr. Young's the night before.

For the next game Evers sets his DVR 'to capture whatever malevolent spirit his past might vomit up.' This time it is a small boy – a schoolmate of Evers transferred in from Tennessee in the spring of 1954. Evers and his buddies mercilessly bullied Lester Embree for his accent, his lack of a live-in father and for his halting answers in class. Embree appears to point a finger directly at Evers and mouth, 'Kill the ump.' Evers recalls the quiet kid being pulled wrinkled and fingerless from Marsden's Pond. That last appears to be a nod to two of the locations in King's fiction – the Marsten House in *'Salem's Lot* and *One for the Road;* and Runaround Pond from *The Dead Zone*. Both are based on locations in Durham, Maine, where King spent his later childhood.

When Evers checks the recording of the game there Embree is – no older than when he'd died decades before, a time when Evers, in a position to stop the bullying of the new boy, had actually ensured its escalation. A week later Embree was fished from the Pond. Now he has returned – looking alive, but with his fingers 'mostly gone', along with some of his nose, as if he has been underwater again. On replay Evers thinks the boy is saying, 'You murdered me.' Evers shouts at the television, *"Not true! You fell in Marsden's! You fell in the pond! You fell in the pond and it was your own goddamned fault!"* He wonders if he's suffering from dementia or having a nervous breakdown.

The next to appear at a game is Evers' dead wife 'wearing the same tennis whites she'd had on the day of her first stroke.' Evers sees her dial her cell phone and his immediately buzzes. He doesn't want to answer but when he does she's on the line. She confirms she's dead and then lays into Evers for an extramarital affair he'd had and thought she hadn't known about; and for the time he'd spent away from her concentrating on his business. She blames him for their son's selfishness, which she claims is learned behavior. As if proving her point, his attention wanders back to the game and, in frustration, Ellie hangs up.

The next strange thing to occur is Evers' old buddy Kaz ringing to complain that Evers hadn't invited him to sit with him in prime seats at that night's baseball game. Evers plays along, even turning up his TV to provide covering sound effects. 'There was only one way to put an end to this cosmic joke. On a Sunday night, downtown St Pete would be deserted. If he took a taxi, he could be at the Trop by the end of the second inning.' The game is a sellout but on a hunch Evers asks for a ticket left in his name at the Will Call window and, sure enough, there's a ticket waiting for him – and one of the best seats in the house at that.

Shortly after being seated Kaz calls again, to tell Evers a cop has reported Evers dead – even though Kaz can see him right there on the television. The cop claimed Evers had been lying dead in his apartment for some time. And now the JumboTron at Tropicana

Field shows Evers stone cold dead in his bedroom. Evers turns his eyes back to the crowd but now the stadium is empty, save for the players and officials continuing the game. After hanging up his call with Kaz, Evers sees ushers bringing in his dead relatives, former employees, girlfriends and acquaintances. 'He couldn't see who'd come to spend eternity with him in peanut heaven or the far reaches of the outfield, but the premium seats were going fast.'

Although clearly an elegiac piece, Evers is portrayed as far from a nice man, indeed one with anger and denial issues, which lends more reality to the tale.

Because the story is collaborative and published as a stand-alone eBook/audio book it is unclear whether King will include *A Face in the Crowd* in a future collection.

Afterlife

Afterlife is a relatively short story, at around 4500 words. It was first published in *Tin House* magazine for Summer 2013 (#56), which can easily be purchased online either direct from the magazine or retailers such as Amazon. We can expect it to appear in King's next short fiction collection.

This story first came to public attention when King read it at 'A Conversation with Stephen King' held at the Tsongas Center of the University of Massachusetts in Lowell, Massachusetts on the evening of 7 December 2012. However, King had mentioned the story title (without any details) as early as 2010. If the YouTube link is still operating you can see King read it at: http://www.youtube.com/watch?v=j--hDgtmQIw&feature=share.

In this New Worlds tale story a man dies and finds himself in a very unusual place and faced with a choice. William Andrews, an investment banker, dies of cancer in 2012. As he passes he sees a white light and then finds himself in a hallway, fit and well, though wearing his pajamas and barefoot. There are only two doors – one is posted as 'Locked' and the other 'Isaac Harris Manager'. He sees a fire extinguisher and a bulletin board with old-style photographs pinned below a sign reading, 'Company Picnic 1956. What Fun We Had!' On examining the photographs a growing sense of unease falls over him as he sees many people from his life but out of context with their ages and careers. He does not recognize most others.

Andrews enters Harris' office where he finds a slightly harried, cynical man who explains that Andrews has visited many times before and always asks the same questions. Initially, Andrews thinks he is to be reincarnated but Harris claims Andrews has entered the manager's own 'afterlife'. Harris and a partner had owned a garment manufacturing operation 'at the turn of the century' and the room represented his own office from 1911. Due to theft and their female workers sneaking out to smoke they had been locked in during their shifts. A fire broke out and, although Harris and his partner escaped, 146 women died, burning to death, falling from a collapsing fire escape, or being killed jumping from ninth and tenth floor windows ('Like 9/11 with fewer casualties,' Andrews commented, to which Harris replied, 'So you always say.') In the subsequent trial the owners were exonerated of blame and Harris still won't accept responsibility when Andrews puts it to him the women died because of his decisions.

Harris' seemingly endless job is to process an ever growing number of souls as they came to his office and offer them the choice of two doors – if they went through one they lived again, through the other they simply vanished into nothingness – an end to their existence. Andrews, like all Harris' pilgrims, initially thinks he can correct some of the mistakes he has made – accidentally injuring his brother, shoplifting on impulse and, worse, the night he took advantage of his drunken date and stood by as two other men also had sex with her. Harris knows of these indiscretions and claims none of his charges can change even one minor aspect of their lives if they return. If they choose the door to oblivion, which he seems to recommend, this actually results in more souls being directed to Harris to process.

Bill Andrews makes his choice, determined to hold on to 'just one thing' he can remember and change. In 1956, Mary Andrews is delivered of a baby boy in Hemingford County Hospital in Nebraska. 'They will name him William, after her paternal grandfather.'

William Andrews was born at Hemingford County Hospital in Nebraska in 1956. One would think that is the county in which Hemingford Home, Nebraska is situated but we are told in *The Stand* that is Polk County. It seems King was intentionally linking this tale to Hemingford Home, which appears in *The Stand, The Last Rung on the Ladder* and *It*.

Bad Little Kid

On March 14, 2014 King published an original story exclusively in French and German, as a thank you to fans who had been so supportive during his tour of those two countries in November the previous year. King confirmed the English title is *Bad Little Kid*[41]. A direct translation of the French title, *Sale Gosse* appears to be *Brat*; and a direct translation of the German title, *Böser kleiner Junge* appears to be *Angry Little Boy*. These French and German editions were e-books only.

One synopsis read, 'George Hallas is in prison. In one week, he is to be executed. He has remained silent for a long time, but now he opens up to his public defender, Leonard Bradley. He tells him how his dreadful deed came to pass. For Bradley, the confession will eventually have spooky consequences.'

The tale is classic King – the antagonist is not only bad but nasty; and the consequences for those who come across him dire. Bradley may regret taking Hallas' confession, which he initially dismisses as implausible, no matter how sane the murderer appears.

We won't go in to a full description here as that would destroy the fun readers will have encountering this tale for the first time. There is no current indication when this 14,800 word story will be published in English but we can be confident that it will be at some stage.

Batman and Robin Have an Altercation

Batman and Robin Have an Altercation is a 4800 word story, which appeared in the prestigious *Harper's Magazine* for September 2012. Copies are held in many libraries and can be sourced from online sellers such as the Overlook Connection and eBay. Set in Texas, this is an America Under Siege tale and we can expect it to appear in the next King short fiction collection.

The story opens with Sanderson visiting his father at the Harvest Hills Special Care Unit (colloquially known as 'Crackerjack Manor'), where he lives after suffering the onset of Alzheimer's Disease. In a few paragraphs King establishes the damage the Disease has done

[41] Personal correspondence, 28 February 2014

to his father's memory and behavior, as well as sketching the elder Sanderson's adult life – first as a 'roughneck in the Texas oilfields'; then, 'civilized' by his new wife, as 'a successful jewelry merchant in San Antonio', a business the younger man has taken over.

Apart from suffering from incontinence and diabetes, Sanderson senior would sometimes erupt into foul language and had developed into a kleptomaniac. Every Sunday the two go out for lunch at a local Applebee's restaurant, where the father always has the same order of chopped steak, and disparagingly compares the dessert to his wife's much superior version. On this particular Sunday 'Pop' confuses his son Dougie with his other son Reggie, run down by a sixteen year old drunk driver forty-five years earlier.

The father remembers he and Dougie had used to love playing Batman and Robin. Dougie recalls the two of them going out for Halloween dressed as 'The Caped Crusader and the Boy Wonder' and tells his father he was 'drunk on your ass and Mom was mad, but I had fun'. This memory pierces the senior's fog and he is able to recall specifics of that night as they drive back to Crackerjack Manor – including that Dougie was 8, so it must have been 1959.

As they roll along the road Dougie is momentarily distracted as his father reminisces. And it is in those few seconds that an accident happens: 'One of those built-up pickup trucks with the oversized tires and the roof-lights on the cab swerves into his lane' and they collide. 'Then he makes a mistake. He pushes the button that unrolls his window, sticks out his arm, and wags his middle finger at the truck.' The other driver gets out and advances – 'he's a south Texas staple. He's wearing jeans and a tee shirt with the sleeves ripped off at the shoulders. Not cut, ripped, so that errant strings dangle against the slabs of muscle on his upper arms. The jeans are hanging off his hipbones so the top two inches of his underwear shows. A chain runs from one beltless loop of his jeans to his back pocket, where there will no doubt be a big leather wallet, possibly embossed with the logo of a heavy metal band. He's got tats on his arms ... They are crude, straggling things: chains around the biceps, thorns around the forearms, a dagger on one wrist with a drop of blood hanging from the tip of the blade. No tattoo parlor did those. That's jailhouse ink. Tat Man is at least six-two in his boots, and at least two hundred pounds. Maybe two-twenty. Sanderson is five-nine and weighs a hundred and sixty.'

Sanderson tries to back down but the other driver is very aggressive, striking the insurance card and registration from his hand; saying he doesn't have insurance, he's leaving and they can both pay for their own damage. Sanderson demands he stay and produce his registration and driver's license. The man immediately punches him: 'There's my registration' and says he doesn't have a license before completely losing it, delivering first a two-handed punch and then kicking Sanderson twice in the side as he lies beside his Subaru. Shocked, Sanderson is unable even to call the man off and is crawling along the blacktop when he notices blood on the road. At first he thinks it's his but then the blood begins to fall *on* him.

He looks up to find a piece of wood sprouting from 'Tat Man's' neck and his father standing beside the assailant, who is suddenly doubled over. At first Dougie doesn't know what he's looking at but it quickly comes to him – his father has stolen the steak knife from Applebee's and buried it in 'Tat Man's' neck. As the wounded man wanders off and drops to his knees the elder man says he was beating on his son and keeps asking who he is. As the sirens begin to wail Dougie helps 'the eighty-three-year-old Caped Crusader into the car'. 'The sixty-one-year-old Boy Wonder' shuffles off to pick up his documents, which the cops will surely want to see.

11/22/63 – Final Dispatch (2012)

King originally wrote a different ending to *11/22/63* but, after a suggestion from his son Joe Hill, wrote the conclusion published in the novel. The moderator of King's official site had this to say about the matter on 20 December 2011:

I've read both of them and have been meaning to ask him if he would consider putting the first version on the site so people could compare. He told me he'd changed it because Joe had seen some problems with the way the first one was written but I don't know with 100% certainty whether Joe gave him specific ideas for the rewrite.

Later:

I was able to ask Steve about this, so here's his answer. Joe only told him that Jake had to meet Sadie again when she was an old lady but how that happened was completely Steve's idea so what we've read in the book was all Steve's writing based on Joe's suggestion to have Jake see Sadie one more time. He also told me it would be okay to put up the original version of the ending but I need to wait at least a month before doing so to give more people the chance to read it as published.

In January 2012 that original chapter, *Final Dispatch* was published at www.stephenking.com. A short piece, it reprints a *Jodie's Doin's* column from the *Kileen Weekly Gazette* of November 22, 2013 (the fiftieth anniversary of John F Kennedy's assassination), and reports on the 50th wedding anniversary celebrations of Sadie Anderson, and her millionaire husband Trevor. A 'man' had found the piece during one of his many Internet searches.

In the Tall Grass

In the Tall Grass is a novella by King and his son, Joe Hill, author of the novels *Heart-Shaped Box, Horns,* and *NOS4A2;* a prize-winning collection of stories, *20th Century Ghosts*; and the comics/graphic novels *Locke & Key* and *Wraith.*

The story was first published in two parts, in *Esquire* magazine for June/July and August 2012[42]; and first appeared in a mass market version as an eBook[43] and audio book in October that same year.

Cal and Becky DeMuth are siblings, born only nineteen months apart, and in synch with each other all their lives. Becky has fallen pregnant, the father is not in the picture, so the two decided to leave New Hampshire and live with their Uncle and Aunt on the West Coast until the baby is born. They are driving through Kansas on an isolated rural road with the windows down and radio off when they hear a kid crying out for help. They immediately pull over – on their side of Route 400 are a few houses, a boarded up church 'called the Black Rock of the Redeemer (which Becky thought a queer name for a church, but this was Kansas)' and a rotting, closed bowling alley. On the far side of the blacktop 'there was nothing but high green grass.'

Listening intently now, they hear faint music from one of the houses, a dog barking and someone hammering on a board. Then,

---

[42] An interview on page 32 of the June/July issue with Hill describes some of the background to the story; and includes some hand-written comments from King. The interview/commentary is quite humorous!

[43] Scribner (US); and The Orion Publishing Group/Hodder & Stoughton (UK)

again, the voice crying for help and "I'm lost!" Looking at the expanse of six foot high grass they are alarmed, it seems like a little kid ('he sounded about eight') had wandered in and become disoriented. The fact that the grass was incredibly high for April was 'an anomaly that wouldn't occur to them until later.' They decide to help and while Becky waits Cal drives their car into the church's dirt parking lot, which held a scattering of 'dust-filmed cars' – 'that all these cars appeared to have been there for days - even weeks - was an another anomaly that would not strike them until later.'

The kid now claims he has been in the grass for days. To Becky he doesn't sound very far in and she is just about to enter the grass when a woman's voice intervenes, "*Don't!* Please! *Stay away*," and asking 'Tobin' to stop calling out – "*He'll hear you!*" Confused, Becky asks what's going on – the boy claims his mother is hurt, the mother tells him again to stop but he persists. Becky suspects if this isn't a prank 'there's something very wrong here' and looks for Cal, seeing him peer into a dust-filmed Prius and flinch at something he sees. Becky climbs down the embankment from the road and notices the grass is even taller than she thought – about seven feet. The boy continues to call her, the mother countermanding him and urging Becky not to look for them. Cal joins her and she explains the situation. The kid sounds close so Cal steps into the grass and is almost immediately lost to Becky's view. She takes out her cell phone, sees she has five bars, dials 9-1-1 and follows Cal in.

The operator answers and Becky tries to explain their location but the operator says it's a bad connection and is then disconnected – the screen is now showing 'NO SERVICE' although she's only a few feet into the grass. The kid starts screaming and there are sounds of a struggle – Cal rushes toward the sound but falls in the wet grass and lands face first in the mud. Cal asks the kid to call out – he again pleads for help but from a different direction than before – how could that be? He looks for his sister but there is nothing but grass – not even the trail of broken down grass where he had walked. Where he had fallen the grass was already springing back. Cal and Becky can talk but not see each other; when Cal jumps he can see the church and road, which seems further away than he expects, but no trace of his sister. Now the kid sounds quite distant

- Cal demands he stand still, to allow them to come to come to him.

Cal decides to find Becky first and gets her to keep talking but their voices constantly seem to be coming from different directions. They agree 'something's wrong here.' And there is – when Becky jumps to glimpse over the grass she sees the road is 140 or so yards away, although she had only walked twenty or thirty steps in. Worse, Cal had jumped at the same time and she briefly glimpsed him ten feet away, although they had to shout to hear each other. And then giddy nervous laughter erupts from a new male voice in the grass. Cal loses it for a few minutes, as his sensory observations and logic clash.

The kid chimes back in, now asking if they'd seen his father, a new player in the mix. Cal tries staying in the same place and jumping thirty seconds later and, sure enough, his location in relation to a sign by the road has undergone a significant change. The strange situation escalates – when Cal falls into the muddy water at the base of the grass the water is hot, as 'hot as bathwater.' Full panic takes hold as he stumbles on a dead dog – flyblown and with maggots boiling in its collapsed stomach cavity, much like the maggots he'd seen on the half-eaten hamburgers on the Prius' passenger seat, back in the church parking lot - someone had left them – and never returned. Calming, he calls Becky and tells her they should try again to find each other by following their voices. And the kid? *"Fuck the kid, Becky! This is about us now!"* And there Part One ends.

Part Two opens with Cal and Becky blundering about trying to find one another, for what seems like hours on end – when Cal checks his watch it has stopped; he thinks the grass has stopped it. Once, Cal thinks the kid is close, and leaping to catch him finds only a dead crow with its head and one wing torn off.

Suddenly the kid's father 'finds' Becky. She screams for him to stay away - that sets Cal into a blind run. The man ('his cheeks were stubbly, his lips red') says he knows how to get out of the grass but Becky sees through that, asking why he was still there if that were the case. He claims he only needs to find his son – he's found his wife Natalie and asks Becky if she wants to meet her. Although she does not trust him and he's clearly mad, Becky feels she has no choice but to follow him. Even though she can hear Cal calling from far away and she knows she should answer she just doesn't have it in her. The madman identifies himself as Ross Humbolt and continues to rave, throwing in a dirty limerick that Becky had thought of earlier. Thinking of self-defense from the maniac she takes the key from their New Hampshire house and sets it between two fingers.

The horror escalates when they reach Ross's wife - dead in the grass – Now Becky knows why Ross' lips were red. Fresh blood on the grass, an arm torn off the body's shoulder with 'divots' in her thighs and one in the discarded arm, all explained by Ross in maniacal terms – the family had been in the grass for a while. "Folks can get pretty hungry ... I'm full now, though." Ross starts rambling about taking Becky to a rock and asking her if she wants to feel it naked, with him in her. Telling her that, if she learns to listen, the grass has things to tell. He claims the rock has taught him many things but "oh, girl, it's so fucking thirsty." A strange lethargy is settling over her as Ross grabs her throat and tightens his grip but she summons enough will to stab him in the face with the house key. The spell broken, she buries the key in his eye – instead of screaming he utters a grunt and attacks her again, kneeing her repeatedly in the stomach, raising her fears for the unborn child. As they struggle his ravings include information he can't possibly know – her surname, their destination of San Diego. Seizing a pair of manicuring scissors that has spilled from the dead woman's purse, she stabs him again and again the face until he first screams, then subsides into 'sobbing guffaws of laughter.' Then silence and Becky's mind goes blank ... until moonrise.

Cal hears all this distantly, without fine detail, as hysteria overtakes him again. When the silence descends he regains control and calls for Becky but receives nothing in reply. When their car alarm sounds it strikes Cal that the locals must know all about the field – perhaps unwary tourists were their sacrifice to it? Tobin appears, eating a dead crow, which Cal snatches from him. Tobin explains that "when you touch the rock you can see", the crows weren't that bad to eat and he hadn't eaten any of Freddy, although his father had. Freddy, he explains, was the family dog. Dead things were easier to find, as the grass didn't move them around. Tobin also informs him that "the rock teaches you to hear the grass, and the tall grass knows everything," before disappearing back into the foliage. Following, Cal finds himself in a clearing – and there is the rock, black, the size of a pickup truck and 'inscribed all over with tiny dancing stick men.' The figures seem to float as Tobin invites Cal to touch the rock.

Becky crawls in the grass, away from Ross, suffering severe cramps. When she is finally able to stop and look, she finds her shorts and panties soaked with blood: *"The baby!"* Unable to control her body, the fetus is delivered – a girl, '...so small. And so silent'.

Cal finds it impossible to determine whether the dancing figures on the rock are above the surface or engraved on it. As he approaches he begins to hear the rock emit a buzzing sound. Tobin tells Cal Becky has miscarried and, when Cal denies this, the boy says he can see her in the rock. Sure enough, a faint image shows Becky's face tormented with pain. Cal feels himself being pulled closer to the rock as if it has its own gravity and finally the rock wins, as Cal presses his face to its cool surface.

Becky dreams of walking out of the grass to the car, then driving through her hometown. She is looking for a girl she's been babysitting, who has wandered off while she had a phone text argument with Travis McKean, the father of her baby. After what seems like days of searching for her charge, she hears a girl calling from some high grass on the other side of a baseball field. She awakes from this nightmare to find Cal beside her, cackling in the grip of madness and holding the dead baby in a tee-shirt. Tobin appears, declaring the baby "scrumptious". Becky loses consciousness and when she comes to sees Cal eating what appears to be a doll's leg, and Tobin licking 'strawberry jelly' from his fingers before darkness claims her again. When she next recovers consciousness Cal is feeding her and she forces the food down as Tobin crows, "Yum, yum. Get that l'il baby right down."

Becky later demands to know what they'd eaten – Cal claims it was just grass but she remembers something salty, tasting like sardines. Her brother and the boy guide her to the rock, she tries to struggle but the rock seems to draw her on – 'She thought: *All flesh is grass.* / Becky DeMuth hugged the rock.'

In the next scene seven latter day hippies in a beat up old RV pull into the church parking lot. They had 'busted mega-amounts of dope and all of them were hungry.' One hears a woman calling from the tall grass on the opposite side of the road, another a little kid calling for help. One of the past middle age women – Ma Cool – surveys the field, which seems to stretch to the horizon and thinks, *I bet all of Kansas looked that way before the people came and spoiled it all.* The group quickly decides they must rescue the people calling for help and once rescued feed them, and all seven plunge into the grass together.

With faint echoes of *Children of the Corn* and recalling the disorientation of King's Lovecraftian tale *N*, this tale is strange and haunting. Hopefully, it will receive a wider readership if published in King's next short fiction collection, or perhaps Hill's.

The Rock and Roll Dead Zone

This amusing little tale (almost a fictional anecdote) was first published in *Hard Listening: The Greatest Rock Band Ever (Of Authors) Tells All*, edited by Sam Barry and Jennifer Lou[44]. The book is an eclectic celebration of the Rock and Roll Remainders, a 'garage band' of writers King has been involved with since 1992. The much better known book about the band is *Mid-Life Confidential: The Rock Bottom Remainders Tour America with Three Chords and an Attitude* edited by Dave Marsh[45].

The story was designed as part of an 'interactive feature' where readers had to guess which of four short stories was written by King. As a result the story doesn't carry King's by-line in the book. Frankly, it wasn't difficult to identify the correct story as King himself is the narrator and protagonist of the tale! The setting is King's home (and he mentions he is a 'poor boy from Maine') so it seems safe to conclude this is a Maine Street Horror tale.

King returns to his home after a tiring book tour, only to find Edward Gooch ('aka Goochie, also aka the Gooch'), a friend since grade school, waiting for him. King loves him 'like a brother' but unfortunately the down on his luck two hundred and eighty pound man has a fascination for bringing outrageously expensive business ideas to 'Steve', some inevitably involving the Gooch's love of rock and roll.

Goochie tells King he could have taken the idea to Dave Barry (another member of the Rock Bottom Remainders) but Steve is a better prospect for 'large concepts'. This idea could

[44] Palo Alto/San Francisco, California: Coliloquy, LLC, June 2013, eBook. ISBN: 978-1-937804-24-4.
[45] New York, New York: Viking Penguin, 1994

cost thirty million dollars! King tries to get rid of his friend, as all he wants to do is rest but ends up promising 'ten minutes'. The Gooch presents his concept via illustrations on cardboard squares – the first is the project's title – 'The Rock and Roll Dead Zone'. "What, exactly, is a rock and roll dead zone? Other than a rip on a book I wrote a thousand years ago?" King asks.

Goochie proceeds through an array of theme park attractions, each worse ideas and puns on songs than the last. Worse still, many are songs long forgotten. One idea is 'a mock up' of the plane 'that Buddy Holly, Richie Valens and J.P. Richardson were riding in'. No matter what King's objections are Goochie has an answer, although none are very good, and he totally misses ironic or sarcastic comments by his author friend. In the meantime King manages to get off some humorous shots at other members of the Rock Bottom Remainders.

Finally, King sees a way out – but you'll have to read the story for that.

This is a terrifically amusing story and King gets to show off some of his encyclopedic knowledge of popular music. It proves again that satire is a mode in which he has all the moves and makes us pine for a few more stories in this vein. It is very unlikely that this story will appear in one of King's mainstream collections as it would lack context and provide a jarring note when juxtaposed against other King tales.

Summer Thunder

This gentle post-apocalyptic New Worlds short story was published in an anthology, *Turn Down the Lights*, edited by Richard Chizmar[46]. It seems to echo *Graduation Afternoon* (both stories involve nuclear attacks on the United States) and *Herman Wouk Is Still Alive* (the theme of suicide). The anthology is available from online booksellers or the publisher, Cemetery Dance Publications, directly.

The story opens with Robinson, who has rescued a dog named Gandalf. The animal's presence was some help dealing with the loss of his wife and daughter. After finding Gandalf he drove to the abandoned and looted country store five miles away to get dog food, which had been left by the looters. It seems that after 'June Sixth, pets had been about the last thing on people's minds.'

---

[46] Cemetery Dance Publications, 2013

Although his wife had stored food at their Vermont lake retreat against 'the apocalypse', she had been in Boston when it came, so Robinson ate for one, knowing the food would last longer. That summer was beautiful but growing silent – his friend Timlin pointed out most birds were gone and Robinson had seen the dead larger animals for himself. When the wind blew from the east the reek of death was tremendous and the heat of summer didn't help – '... Robinson wanted to know what had happened to nuclear winter.'

Each day Robinson walked the dog over to Howard Timlin's place two miles away at Woodland Acres, once a pricey gated tourist spot with up-scale 'cottages'. The owners had swallowed pills in early July, leaving Timlin the sole survivor in residence. The walk was picturesque, with views from the road high above the lake. 'At one point, where the road buttonhooked sharply' a sign advised caution to drivers; 'the summer kids of course called this hairpin Dead Man's Curve'.

The two men talked of the past and their limited future – Robinson the more sanguine of the two; Timlin the doomsayer - constantly searched for signs of radiation poisoning, finding a patch of the dog's fur which came out easily when pulled and reporting that he'd lost a tooth. Timlin also enquired after Robinson's motorcycle, which he had promised his wife he would sell when he turned fifty. An empty promise now that all the cities of the Eastern seaboard, including Boston were 'now mostly slag'. Anyway, the bike's battery was dead.

On the way home Gandalf collapsed and was clearly dying later that evening: 'It's happening so fast,' he [Robinson] thought. 'This morning he was fine.' Robinson went out to the lean-to to inspect the motorcycle – a 2014 Fat Bob, 'several years old now'. By the morning Gandalf was much worse but Robinson decided to head into Bennington in his Silverado to see if he could find a replacement battery for the motorcycle. Dropping into Timlin's to ask if he needed anything he found his friend very ill and, although he said he didn't need anything, asked Robinson to drop by on the return trip as he had something Robinson might want.

In Bennington, Robinson found a live battery at the local Harley-Davidson franchise. Returning, he found Timlin in a worse state and preparing to commit suicide: 'Robinson recognized the absurdity of the first thing that came to mind – Let's not be hasty

– and managed to stay silent.' Timlin intended to shoot himself and offered Robinson a hypo of Demerol to euthanize Gandalf.

When Robinson got home he found Gandalf still alive, happy to see his new master but unable to get up. As Robinson prepared to give the dog his final injection he heard the faint sound of a single gunshot roll across the lake. Robinson administered the injection 'and in the endless moment before the brightness left [Gandalf's eyes], Robinson would have taken it back if he could.' He buried the dog and next morning awoke to find his gums and nose had bled in the night.

Robinson replaced the motor cycle's battery, 'hit the ignition and the sound of summer thunder shattered the quiet.' He mounted the bike and rolled out the driveway and onto the road, building up speed on a straight stretch. Seeing the safety sign denoting Dead Man's Curve he 'aimed for the sign and twisted the throttle all the way. He just had time to hit fifth gear.'

AFTERWORD

And that is the end of King's new fiction for now. Stephen King is now 66 but shows no signs of slowing down. We can expect at least a novel a year for some years, and probably two to four short stories every twelve months as well.

King researchers continue our search for the lost stories – as we can see from this update volume they are still to be found.

So, Constant Readers, enjoy!

Melbourne, Australia

19 March 2014

Appendix: Stephen King's Fiction

The following is a list of all known King fiction published or announced as at 19 March 2014. Where the author of this volume has assessed that the story appears in different versions or variations (*see Chapter 4* of *Stephen King: Uncollected, Unpublished*, Fourth Edition – *Variations and Versions in King's Fiction* for more detail) these are listed individually. Otherwise, only the first point of publication and any inclusions in a King collection are listed.

The codes used below are: (a) = Abridgement; (e) = Excerpt (n) = New Version; (r) = Reprint; (v) = Variation.

Afterlife — *Tin House,* Summer 2013

The Aftermath — Unpublished Novel

All That You Love Will Be Carried Away — *The New Yorker,* 29 January 2001

All That You Love Will Be Carried Away — *Everything's Eventual* (v)

American Vampire — Graphic Novel

An Evening at God's — Unpublished Play

Apt Pupil — *Different Seasons*

Autopsy Room Four — *Six Stories*

Autopsy Room Four — *Everything's Eventual* (r)

Ayana — *Paris Review,* Fall 2007

Ayana — *Just After Sunset* (r)

Bad Little Kid — eBook in French and German

Bag of Bones — Novel

The Ballad of the Flexible Bullet — *The Magazine of Fantasy and Science Fiction,* June 1984

The Ballad of the Flexible Bullet — *Secret Windows*

Batman — Unpublished Play

Batman and Robin Have an Altercation — Harper's Magazine, September 2012

Battleground — Cavalier, September 1972

Battleground — Night Shift (v)

Battleground — Night Shift Screenplay (n)

Beachworld — Weird Tales, Fall 1984

Beachworld – Skeleton Crew (v)

The Bear - The Magazine of Fantasy and Science Fiction, December 1990

The Bear - The Dark Tower III: The Waste Lands (n)

Before the Play — Whispers, August 1982

Before the Play — TV Guide, 26 April – 2 May 1997 (a)

The Beggar and the Diamond - Nightmares and Dreamscapes

Beneath the Demon Moon — Paperback Giveaway

Beneath the Demon Moon — The Dark Tower IV: Wizard and Glass

Big Driver — Full Dark, No Stars

Big Wheels - A Tale of the Laundry Game (Milkman #2) - New Terrors 2

Big Wheels - A Tale of the Laundry Game (Milkman #2) - Skeleton Crew (n)

The Bird and the Album — A Fantasy Reader: The Seventh World Fantasy Convention Program Book

The Bird and the Album - It (n)

Black House — Novel

Black Ribbons — Black Ribbons (album), *2010*

Blaze — Novel

Blind Willie — Antaeus, Autumn 1994

Blind Willie — Six Stories (v)

Blind Willie — Hearts in Atlantis (n)

Blockade Billy — Novella

The Blue Air Compressor — Onan, January 1971

The Blue Air Compressor — Heavy Metal, July 1981 (v)

The Body — Different Seasons

The Bone Church — Playboy, November 2009

The Boogeyman — Cavalier, March 1973

The Boogeyman — Night Shift (v)

The Breathing Method — Different Seasons

Brooklyn August — Io, 1971

Brooklyn August — Nightmares and Dreamscapes (r)

But Only Darkness Loves Me — Unpublished Short Story

Cain Rose Up — Ubris, Spring 1968

Cain Rose Up — Skeleton Crew (n)

Calla Bryn Sturgis — www.stephenking.com

Calla Bryn Sturgis — The Dark Tower V: Wolves of the Calla (n)

The Cannibals — www.stephenking.com

Carrie — Novel

The Cat From Hell — Cavalier, June 1977

The Cat From Hell — Just After Sunset

Cat's Eye — Unpublished Screenplay

Cell — Novel

Chapter 71 – Sword in the Darkness — Stephen King: Uncollected, Unpublished

Charlie — Unpublished Short Story

Chattery Teeth — Cemetery Dance, Fall 1992

Chattery Teeth — Nightmares and Dreamscapes (n)

Children of the Corn — Penthouse, March 1977

Children of the Corn — Night Shift (n)

Children of the Corn — Unpublished Screenplay (n)

Chinga — Unpublished Screenplay

Chip Coombs — Unpublished Story

Christine — Novel

Code Name: Mousetrap — *The Drum,* 27 October 1965

The Colorado Kid — Novel

Comb Dump — Unpublished Story

The Crate — *Gallery,* July 1979

The Crate — *Creepshow* Screenplay (n)

The Crate — *Creepshow* (n)

Creepshow — Unpublished Screenplay

Crouch End — *New Tales of the Cthulhu Mythos*

Crouch End — *Nightmares and Dreamscapes* (n)

Cujo — *Novel*

Cujo — Unpublished Screenplay (n)

The Cursed Expedition — *People, Places and Things*

Cycle of the Werewolf — Novella

The Dark Half — Novel

The Dark Man — *Ubris,* Fall 1969

The Dark Man – Illustrated Book

The Dark Tower: The Gunslinger — Original Novel

The Dark Tower: The Gunslinger — Revised and Expanded Novel (n)

The Dark Tower II: The Drawing of the Three — Novel

The Dark Tower III: The Wastelands — Novel

The Dark Tower IV: Wizard and Glass — Novel

The Dark Tower V: Wolves of the Calla — Novel

The Dark Tower VI: Song of Susannah — Novel

The Dark Tower VII: The Dark Tower — Novel

The Dead Zone — Novel

The Dead Zone — Unpublished Screenplay (n)

The Death of Jack Hamilton — *The New Yorker,* 24/31 December 2001

The Death of Jack Hamilton — *Everything's Eventual* (r)

Dedication — *Night Visions 5*

Dedication — *Nightmares and Dreamscapes* (n)

Desperation — Novel

Desperation — Unpublished Screenplay (n)

Dino — *The Salt Hill Journal,* Autumn 1994

The Doctor's Case — *The New Adventures of Sherlock Holmes*

The Doctor's Case — *Nightmares and Dreamscapes (r)*

Do the Dead Sing? — *Yankee,* November 1981

Dolan's Cadillac — *Castle Rock,* 1985

Dolan's Cadillac — Limited Edition Novella (n)

Dolan's Cadillac — *Nightmares and Dreamscapes* (r)

Dolan's Cadillac — Unpublished Screenplay (v)

Dolores Claiborne — Novel

Donovan's Brain — *Moth,* 1970

Dreamcatcher — Novel

Duma Key — Novel

The Dune — *Granta* magazine, Fall/Winter 2011

11/22/63 — Novel

11/22/63 – Final Despatch - www.stephenking.com

The End of the Whole Mess — *Omni,* October 1986

The End of the Whole Mess — *Nightmares and Dreamscapes* (n)

The Evaluation — Unpublished Story

Everything's Eventual — *The Magazine of Fantasy and Science Fiction,* October 1997

Everything's Eventual — *F13* (v)

Everything's Eventual — *Everything's Eventual* (v)

Eyes of the Dragon — Limited Edition Novel

Eyes of the Dragon — Mass Market Novel (n)

A Face in the Crowd — Electronic book

Fair Extension — *Full Dark, No Stars*

The Falls of the Hounds — Paperback Giveaway

The Falls of the Hounds — *The Dark Tower IV: Wizard and Glass*

Father's Day — *Creepshow* Screenplay

Father's Day — *Creepshow* (n)

The Fifth Quarter — *Cavalier,* April 1972

The Fifth Quarter — *The Twilight Zone Magazine,* February 1986 (n)

The Fifth Quarter — *Nightmares and Dreamscapes* (n)

Firestarter — Novel

For Owen — *Skeleton Crew*

For the Birds — *Bred Any Good Rooks Lately?*

The 43rd Dream — *The Drum,* 29 January 1966

The 43rd Dream — *The Illustrated Stephen King Companion*

Blood and Smoke — *Everything's Eventual* (v)

From a Buick 8 — Novel

The Furnace — *Know Your World Extra*

General — *Screamplays*

George D X McArdle — Unpublished Novel

Gerald's Game — Novel

Ghost Brothers of Darkland County — Libretto

The Gingerbread Girl — *Esquire,* July 2007

The Gingerbread Girl — *Just After Sunset*

The Girl Who Loved Tom Gordon — Novel

The Glass Floor — Startling Mystery Stories, Fall 1967

The Glass Floor — Weird Tales, Fall 1990 (v)

Golden Years — Unpublished Screenplay

A Good Marriage — Full Dark, No Stars

Graduation Afternoon — Postscripts, Spring 2007

Graduation Afternoon — Just After Sunset (r)

Gramma — Weirdbook, Spring 1984

Gramma — Skeleton Crew (n)

Graveyard Shift — Cavalier, October 1970

Graveyard Shift — Night Shift (r)

Gray Matter — Cavalier, October 1973

Gray Matter — Night Shift (r)

The Green Mile — Serialized Novel

The Green Mile — Omnibus Novel (v)

The Hardcase Speaks — Contraband, 1 December 1971

Harrison State Park '68 — Ubris, Fall 1968

Harvey's Dream — The New Yorker, 30 June 2003

Harvey's Dream — Just After Sunset (r)

Hearts in Atlantis — Hearts in Atlantis

Heavenly Shades of Night Are Falling — Hearts in Atlantis

Here There Be Tygers — Ubris, Spring 1968

Here There Be Tygers — Skeleton Crew (v)

Heroes for Hope Starring the X-Men — Heroes for Hope Starring the X-Men, #1

Home Delivery — The Book of the Dead

Home Delivery — Nightmares and Dreamscapes (n)

The Hotel at the End of the Road — People, Places and Things

The House on Maple Street — Nightmares and Dreamscapes

I Am the Doorway — Cavalier, March 1971

I Am the Doorway — *Night Shift* (r)

I Hate Mondays — Unpublished Short Story

I Know What You Need — *Cosmopolitan,* September 1976

I Know What You Need — *Night Shift* (v)

I Know What You Need — *Night Shift* Screenplay (n)

The Insanity Game — Unpublished short story

Insomnia — Novel

In the Deathroom — *Blood and Smoke*

In the Deathroom — *Secret Windows: Essays and Fiction on the Craft of Writing* (v)

In the Deathroom — *Everything's Eventual* (v)

In the key-chords of dawn — *Onan,* 1971

In The Tall Grass — *Esquire,* June/July & August 2012

It — Novel

It Grows on You — *Marshroots,* Fall 1973

It Grows on You — *Weird Tales,* Summer 1991 (v)

It Grows on You — *Whispers,* July 1982 (n)

It Grows on You — *Nightmares and Dreamscapes* (n)

I've Got to Get Away — *People, Places and Things*

I Was a Teenage Grave Robber — *Comics Review,* 1965

As *In a Half-World of Terror* — *Stories of Suspense,* 1966 (n)

The Jaunt — *The Twilight Zone Magazine,* June 1981

The Jaunt — *Skeleton Crew* (n)

Jerusalem's Lot — *Night Shift*

Jhonathan and the Witchs — *First Words: Earliest Writing from Favorite Contemporary Authors*

Jumper — *Dave's Rag,* Winter 1959-1960

Jumper — *Secret Windows: Essays and Fiction on the Craft of Writing* (r)

Keyholes — Unpublished Short Story

The Killer — *Famous Monsters of Filmland,* Spring 1994

Kingdom Hospital — Unpublished Screenplay

The King Family and the Wicked Witch — *Flint,* 25 August 1977

The Langoliers — *Four Past Midnight*

The Last Rung on the Ladder — *Night Shift*

The Lawnmower Man — *Cavalier,* May 1975

The Lawnmower Man — *Night Shift* (v)

The Lawnmower Man — *Bizarre Adventures,* October 1981 (n)

The Ledge — *Penthouse,* July 1976

The Ledge — *Night Shift* (v)

The Ledge - Cat's Eye Screenplay (n)

The Leprechaun — Unpublished Novel

The Library Policeman — *Four Past Midnight*

The Little Green God of Agony — *A Book of Horrors*

The Little Sisters of Eluria — *Legends: Short Novels by the Masters of Modern Fantasy*

The Little Sisters of Eluria — *Everything's Eventual* (v)

Lisey and Amanda (Everything the Same) — *Cell,* 2006

Lisey and Amanda (Everything the Same) — *Lisey's Story,* 2006 (v)

Lisey and the Madman — *McSweeney's Enchanting Chamber of Astonishing Stories*

Lisey and the Madman — *Lisey's Story,* 2006 (v)

Lisey's Story — Novel

The Lonesome Death of Jordy Verrill — *Creepshow* Screenplay

The Lonesome Death of Jordy Verrill — *Creepshow* (n)

The Long Walk — Novel

Low Men in Yellow Coats — *Hearts in Atlantis*

Low Men in Yellow Coats — *Family Circle* (v)

L T's Theory of Pets — *Six Stories*

L T's Theory of Pets — *Everything's Eventual* (v)

The Luckey Quarter — *USA Weekend,* 30 June – 2 July 1995

The Luckey Quarter — *Six Stories* (n)

The Luckey Quarter — *Everything's Eventual* (r)

Lunch at the Gotham Café — *Dark Love*

Lunch at the Gotham Café — *Six Stories* (n)

Lunch at the Gotham Café — *Blood and Smoke* (r)

Lunch at the Gotham Café — *Everything's Eventual* (v)

The Man in the Black Suit — *The New Yorker,* 31 October 1994

The Man in the Black Suit — *Six Stories* (v)

The Man in the Black Suit — *Everything's Eventual* (v)

The Man Who Loved Flowers — *Gallery,* August 1977

The Man Who Loved Flowers — *Night Shift* (v)

The Man Who Would Not Shake Hands — *Shadows 4*

The Man Who Would Not Shake Hands — *Skeleton Crew* (n)

Man With A Belly — *Cavalier,* December 1978

The Mangler — *Cavalier,* December 1972

The Mangler — *Night Shift* (v)

Maximum Overdrive — Unpublished Screenplay

Memory — *Tin House,* Summer 2006

Memory — *Duma Key* (v)

Mile 81 — e-book

Misery — Novel

The Mist — *Dark Forces*

The Mist — *Skeleton Crew* (n)

Mr. Mercedes — Novel

Mobius — Unpublished Story

Molly — Unpublished Screenplay

The Monkey — *Gallery,* November 1980

The Monkey — *Skeleton Crew* (n)

The Monster in the Closet — *Ladies Home Journal,* October 1981 (v)

The Monster in the Closet - Cujo

Morality — *Esquire,* July 2009

Morality — *Blockade Billy*

Morning Deliveries (Milkman #1) — *Skeleton Crew*

Mostly Old Men — *Tin House,* Summer 2009

Movie Show — Unpublished Story

The Moving Finger — *The Magazine of Fantasy and Science Fiction,* December 1990

The Moving Finger — *Nightmares and Dreamscapes* (n)

Mrs. Todd's Shortcut — *Redbook*

Mrs. Todd's Shortcut — *Skeleton Crew* (v)

Muffe — Unpublished story

Muffe — *The Stephen King Illustrated Companion*

Mute — *Playboy,* December 2007

Mute — *Just After Sunset* (r)

My Pretty Pony — Limited/Trade Novella

My Pretty Pony — *Nightmares and Dreamscapes* (n)

N — *Just After Sunset* (r)

Needful Things — Novel

Never Look Behind You — *People, Places and Things*

The New Lieutenant's Rap — Limited Edition Chapbook

The New York Times at Special Bargain Rates — *The Magazine of Fantasy & Science Fiction,* October/November 2008

The New York Times at Special Bargain Rates — *Just After Sunset* (r)

The Night Flier — *Prime Evil: New Stories by the Masters of Modern Fiction*

The Night Flier — *Nightmares and Dreamscapes* (n)

The Night of the Tiger — *The Magazine of Fantasy and Science Fiction*, February 1978

Night Shift — Unpublished Screenplay

Night Surf — *Ubris*, Spring 1969

Night Surf — *Cavalier*, August 1974 (n)

Night Surf — *Night Shift* (v)

1922 - Full Dark, No Stars

Nona — *Shadows*

Nona — *Skeleton Crew* (n)

The Null Set — Unpublished short story

The Old Dude's Ticker — *Necon XX Commemorative Volume*

One for the Road — *Maine*, March/April 1977

One for the Road — *Night Shift* (v)

As *Return to 'Salem's Lot* — *Vampire Omnibus* (v)

The Other Side of the Fog — *People, Places and Things*

Paranoid: A Chant — *Skeleton Crew*

Pet Sematary — Novel

Pet Sematary — Unpublished Screenplay (n)

Phil and Sundance — Unpublished Novel

The Plant — Incomplete Novel in Three Parts

The Plant — Incomplete Novel in Six Parts (n)

The Points Dig Deep — Unpublished Short Story

Popsy — *Masques II*

Popsy — *Nightmares and Dreamscapes* (n)

The Pulse — www.amazon.com

The Pulse — *Cell* (n)

Premium Harmony — The New Yorker, 9 November 2009

Quitters, Inc. — Night Shift

Quitters, Inc. — Cat's Eye Screenplay (n)

The Raft — Gallery, November 1982

The Raft — Skeleton Crew (v)

Rage — Novel

Rainy Season — Midnight Graffiti, Spring 1989

Rainy Season — Nightmares and Dreamscapes (n)

The Reach — Skeleton Crew

The Reaper's Image — Startling Mystery Stories, Spring 1969

The Reaper's Image — Skeleton Crew (v)

The Regulators — Novel

The Reploids — Unpublished Novel

The Reploids — Night Visions 5

Rest Stop — Esquire, December 2003

Rest Stop — Just After Sunset (r)

The Return of Timmy Baterman — Satyricon II Program Book

The Return of Timmy Baterman — Pet Sematary (v)

The Revelations of 'Becka Paulson — Rolling Stone, 19 July/
   2 August 1984

The Revelations of 'Becka Paulson — Skeleton Crew (Limited) (r)

The Revelations of 'Becka Paulson — The Tommyknockers (n)

Revival — As yet Unpublished Novel (due November 2014)

The Revenge of Lard Ass Hogan — Maine Review, July 1975

The Revenge of Lard Ass Hogan — The Body (n)

Riding the Bullet — Electronic Book

Riding the Bullet — Everything's Eventual (r)

Rita Hayworth and Shawshank Redemption — Different Seasons

The Road Virus Heads North - 999

The Road Virus Heads North — *Everything's Eventual* (n)

Roadwork — Novel

Rose Madder — Novel

Rose Red — Unpublished Screenplay

The Running Man — Novel

Rush Call — *Dave's Rag,* Winter 1959-1960

Rush Call — *Secret Windows: Essays and Fiction on the Craft of Writing* (r)

'Salem's Lot — Novel

'Salem's Lot — Novel (v) *Centipede Press edition*

Secret Window, Secret Garden — *Four Past Midnight*

The Shining — Novel

The Shining — Unpublished Movie Screenplay (n)

The Shining — Unpublished Mini-Series Screenplay (n)

The Shotgunners — Unpublished Screenplay

Silence — *Moth,* 1970

Silver Bullet — Screenplay

Skybar — *The Do-It-Yourself Bestseller – A Workbook*

Slade — *The Maine Summer Campus,* 1970

Sleepwalkers — Unpublished Screenplay

Sneakers — *Night Visions 5*

Sneakers — *Nightmares and Dreamscapes* (n)

Something to Tide You Over — *Creepshow* Screenplay

Something to Tide You Over — *Creepshow* (n)

Something Wicked This Way Comes — Unpublished Screenplay

Sometimes They Come Back — *Cavalier,* March 1974

Sometimes They Come Back — *Night Shift* (v)

Sorry, Right Number — Unpublished Shooting Script

Sorry, Right Number — *Nightmares and Dreamscapes* (n)

Squad D — Unpublished Short Story

The Stand — Original Novel

The Stand — Original Novel (v)

The Stand — Complete and Uncut Novel (n)

The Stand — Unpublished Movie Screenplay (n)

The Stand — Unpublished Mini-Series Screenplay (n)

The Star Invaders — Unpublished Short Story

Stationary Bike — *Borderlands 5*

Stationary Bike — *Just After Sunset* (r)

Storm of the Century — Screenplay

The Stranger — *People, Places and Things*

Strawberry Spring — *Ubris,* Fall 1968

Strawberry Spring — *Cavalier,* November 1975 (n)

Strawberry Spring — *Night Shift* (r)

Strawberry Spring — *Night Shift* Screenplay (n)

Stud City — *Ubris,* Fall 1969

Stud City — *The Body* (n)

Suffer the Little Children — *Cavalier,* February 1972

Suffer the Little Children — *Nightmares and Dreamscapes* (n)

Summer Thunder — *Turn Down the Lights*

The Sun Dog — *Four Past Midnight*

Survivor Type — *Terrors*

Survivor Type — *Skeleton Crew* (v)

Sword in the Darkness — Unpublished Novel

The Tale of Gray Dick — *Timothy McSweeney's Quarterly Concern,* 25 February 2003

The Tale of Gray Dick — *The Dark Tower V: Wolves of the Calla* (v)

The Talisman — Novel

The Ten O'Clock People — *Nightmares and Dreamscapes*

That Feeling, You Can Only Say What It Is In French — *The New Yorker,* 22/29 June 1998

That Feeling, You Can Only Say What It Is In French — *Everything's Eventual* (v)

They're Creeping Up on You — *Creepshow* Screenplay

They're Creeping Up on You — *Creepshow* (n)

The Thing at the Bottom of the Well — *People, Places and Things*

The Things They Left Behind — *Transgressions*

The Things They Left Behind — *Just After Sunset* (r)

Thinner — Novel

Throttle — *He Is Legend: An Anthology Celebrating Richard Matheson*

Tommy — *Playboy,* March 2010

The Tommyknockers — Novel

Trucks — *Cavalier,* June 1973

Trucks — *Night Shift* (v)

Umney's Last Case — *Nightmares and Dreamscapes*

Uncle Otto's Truck — *Yankee,* October 1983

Uncle Otto's Truck — *Skeleton Crew* (n)

Under the Dome — Novel

Under the Weather — *Full Dark, No Stars* (paperback only)

Untitled — Self-published story (c.1957/58)

Untitled — Unpublished Story Fragment (2002)

Untitled (The Huffman Story) — Unpublished Novel

Untitled (She Has Gone to Sleep While) — *Contraband,* 31 October 1971

Untitled Play — Unpublished Script (1959/60)

Untitled Screenplay (Radio Station) — Unpublished Screenplay

Untitled Under the Dome episode — Unpublished Teleplay

Ur — www.amazon.com, 12 February 2009

A Very Tight Place — *McSweeney's Quarterly Concern*, May 2008

The Wedding Gig — *Ellery Queen's Mystery Magazine*, December 1980

The Wedding Gig — *Skeleton Crew* (n)

Weeds — *Cavalier*, May 1976

What Tricks Your Eye — Unpublished Story

Why We're in Vietnam — *Hearts in Atlantis*

Willa — *Playboy*, December 2006

Wimsey — Unpublished Novel

The Wind Through the Keyhole — Novel

The Woman in the Room — *Night Shift*

Woman with Child — *Contraband*, 31 October 1971

The Word Processor — *Playboy*, January 1983

Word Processor of the Gods — *Skeleton Crew*

You Know They Got a Hell of a Band — *Shock Rock*

You Know They Got a Hell of a Band — *Nightmares and Dreamscapes* (n)

Non Fiction

King's contribution to non-fiction is often overlooked due to his huge output of fiction. However, he has actually been responsible for nearly 900 separate pieces of non-fiction through February 2014, ranging from entire books to short articles, reviews and the like.

The most extensive review of these ever compiled (including even such minor items as letters to the editor) appears in *Stephen King: The Non-Fiction* by Rocky Wood and Justin Brooks (Cemetery Dance, 2009). The authors spent five years compiling this reference work, with the assistance of many of the leading King researchers, collectors and 'super-collectors'; and access to the Restricted Non-Fiction Works in King's papers at the Raymond H Fogler Library of the University of Maine, Orono.

Covering all King's published and known unpublished works from 1959 through late 2006, *Stephen King: The Non-Fiction* revealed *for the first time* dozens of pieces of non-fiction and their appearances that were previously unknown to King researchers.

About the Author

Rocky Wood was my go-to guy for all things Shining, providing me with names and dates I had either forgotten or plain got wrong. He also provided reams of info on every recreational vehicle and camper under the sun (the coolest was Rose's EarthCruiser). The Rock knows my work better than I do myself. Look him up on the web sometime. He's got it going on.

Stephen King in the *Author's Note to Doctor Sleep*

Rocky Wood lives in Melbourne, Australia and is the author of major works about Stephen King. Three of these were nominated for the Horror Writers Association's Bram Stoker Award® for Superior Achievement in Non-Fiction – *Stephen King: Uncollected, Unpublished, Stephen King: The Non-Fiction,* and *Stephen King: The Literary Companion,* which won the 2011 Award.

He is also the author of two graphic novels, including *Witch Hunts! A Graphic History of the Burning Times*, which won the 2012 Bram Stoker Award for Superior Achievement in a Graphic Novel.

A freelance journalist since the 1970s, his articles have been published all over the world, including on subjects such as UFOs, the security industry and popular culture. His website is at www.rockywoodauthor.com.

He has spoken at numerous conventions, including the SKEMER Con in Estes Park, Colorado (2003); Continuum 3 (2005) and Continuum 4 (2006) in Melbourne; Conflux 3 in Canberra (2006); the 2nd Annual Stephen King Dollar Baby Festival in Bangor, Maine (2005), the World Horror Conventions in Salt Lake City (2008) and Austin (2011); the Bram Stoker Award Weekends (Burbank, 2009; Long Island, 2011; and New Orleans 2013); Worldcon in Melbourne (2010); was a Special Guest at the World Horror Convention in Salt Lake City (2012); and has even addressed Stephen King's hometown Historical Society about the author's works and motivations. He was Chair of the World Horror Convention 2013, held in New Orleans.

Rocky has undertaken seven research trips to Maine, rediscovering many previously lost or unknown pieces written by King; and is recognized as one of the world's leading experts on King's work.

He served as a Trustee of the Horror Writers Association (HWA) from 2008 to 2010; was elected President of the HWA in 2010, and re-elected in 2012 and 2014. He is also an Active member of the International Thriller Writers and a founding member of the Australian Horror Writers Association.

He met with Stephen King in Atlanta in April 2012 and thanks the master for all the help he has provided to his research over the years.

Rocky was born and grew up in Wellington, New Zealand. Apart from his Australian citizenship he is also a proud New Zealander, particularly when it comes to sport. In fact he's a bit of a sports nut. He has a passion for Rugby Union (and was in the crowd when the All Blacks won both of their World Cups), in which he supports the All Blacks, the Wellington Hurricanes, and the Wellington Lions; Association Football (Soccer), in which he supports Manchester United (and was fortunate to be at Old Trafford to see the Red Devils vanquish Liverpool in 2010 and to see Wayne Rooney score); Baseball, in which he supports the Boston Red Sox (he has been to Fenway for a number of games, even seeing David Ortiz hit a game-winning home run); and Cricket, in which he generally suffers from supporting the Black Caps (although he does remember the Glory Days of Hadlee, et al and was at the Basin Reserve when New Zealand first beat England in a Test Match).

Rocky has had a long term love affair with the United States and its history. He has visited the country around 50 times over 35 years, indulging his passion for (almost) all things American, particularly the Civil War. A long-time supporter of Australia's Alliance with the US, he was President of the Australian American Association of Victoria (founded by Sir Keith Murdoch) from 2008–2010 and was elected a Life Member in September 2010.

His professional career concentrated in the Logistics Industry, having had senior leadership roles with UPS, TNT, Australia Post and Telstra. He was a member of the Australian Logistics Council (the industry's peak body) from 2008 to 2012.

An inveterate traveler, he has lived in New Zealand, Australia,

Belgium and England and has been seen visiting much of the world - only the continent of Antarctica has escaped his tread (although he flew over it on a tourist flight – a unique and awe-inspiring experience).

In the 1970s and 1980s Rocky was deeply involved in research into the theory that our planet has been visited in the past by extra-terrestrials and had the good fortune to spend time travelling with Erich von Daniken, author of *Chariots of the Gods?* and many other books. Erich even signed Rocky's first edition copy of that book atop the Temple of the Inscriptions in Palenque, Mexico (the tombstone from the pyramid features on the cover of the book). During this time he spoke at a number of Conventions including the 5th World Conference of the Ancient Astronaut Society (Chicago, 1978); the 7th World Conference of the AAS (Auckland, 1980) and the MUFON Conference in San Francisco (1979). He even met Dr. J Allen Hynek, the man who coined the term 'Close Encounters of the Third Kind' in his classic book, *The UFO Experience.*

He is also the proud father of two daughters – Alicia and Natasha, and a grand-daughter, Bailie.

In October 2010 Rocky was diagnosed with Motor Neurone Disease (MND) or Amyotrophic Lateral Sclerosis (ALS), also known as Lou Gehrig's Disease. The disorder causes muscle weakness and atrophy throughout the body caused by the degeneration of the upper and lower motor neurons. Unable to function, the muscles weaken and atrophy. Individuals affected by the disorder may ultimately lose the ability to initiate and control almost all voluntary movement. Patients progress differently but about 95% die within 3-5 years of being diagnosed. There is no treatment for the underlying disease (only for the symptoms) and no cure. Rocky encourages you to learn more about this disease and contribute to your local support groups and research charities. In the US a good place to start is http://www.alsa.org/. In Australia please visit: http://www.mndaust.asn.au/.

www.ingramcontent.com/pod-product-compliance
Lightning Source LLC
Chambersburg PA
CBHW061156040426
42445CB00013B/1701